CYBER
SECURITY
RISKS
AND CONTROLS

FUNDAMENTALS OF
ORGANIZATIONAL CYBERSECURITY

DR IAN MESSENGER

Copyright © 2024 by Dr Ian Messenger

CYBERSECURITY RISKS AND CONTROLS

Interior Design and Formatting: Nonon Tech & Design

ISBN: 978-1-7380088-9-6 (Paperback)
ISBN: 978-1-7380088-8-9 (Hardback)

TABLE OF CONTENTS

INTRODUCTION TO CYBERSECURITY

In an age dominated by digital landscapes and interconnected technologies, the term "cybersecurity" has emerged as a critical guardian of our online spaces. At its core, cybersecurity represents a fortress of defense against the ever-evolving landscape of digital threats that lurk in the shadows of the online world. It encompasses a vast array of strategies, technologies, and practices designed to safeguard our digital existence from malicious actors seeking to exploit vulnerabilities for various nefarious purposes. Picture it as the digital armor that shields our sensitive information, critical infrastructure, and personal data from the prying eyes of cybercriminals.

To truly grasp the importance of cybersecurity, one must first navigate the intricate terrain of cybersecurity threats – an ensemble of sophisticated challenges that range from malware and phishing attacks to more intricate forms of cyber espionage. As we embark on this journey, we'll unravel the complex web of cybersecurity concepts and terminology, demystifying the cryptic language that often shrouds this field. Moreover, we'll delve into the pressing need for robust cybersecurity measures in a world where the boundaries between the physical and digital are becoming increasingly blurred. In essence, understanding and embracing cybersecurity isn't merely a choice; it's an imperative response to the omnipresent risks that accompany our interconnected digital existence.

In the vast digital expanse that defines our modern era, understanding cybersecurity threats is akin to deciphering a complex puzzle where the stakes are high, and the adversaries are often elusive. Imagine navigating a bustling city, each corner hiding potential risks and unseen dangers. Similarly, the digital realm is teeming with threats that exploit vulnerabilities in our interconnected systems. One of the most common adversaries comes in the form of malware – malicious software designed to infiltrate and damage computer systems. Picture it as a silent infiltrator, capable of wreaking havoc on your personal files or even holding them hostage for ransom.

Phishing, another subtle yet pervasive threat, involves deceptive tactics to trick individuals into revealing sensitive information such as passwords or credit card details. It's like a cunning con artist who, through clever disguises, gains access to your personal fortress. Cyber espionage, a more sophisticated menace, involves state or corporate-sponsored actors engaging in covert activities to pilfer sensitive information. It's akin to digital spies infiltrating virtual borders, stealing valuable secrets without leaving a trace.

The landscape is also plagued by Distributed Denial- Of-Service (DDoS) attacks, where a flood of traffic overwhelms a system, rendering it inaccessible. Imagine a swarm of traffic converging on a single road, causing a gridlock and preventing anyone from passing through. This disruption can paralyze businesses, disrupt services, and create chaos in the digital ecosystem.

As technology advances, so do the threats. The rise of the Internet of Things (IoT) introduces new vulnerabilities. Consider smart devices in homes – from thermostats to security cameras. If not adequately protected, these devices can become entry points for cyber intruders, turning our homes into digital battlegrounds.

Social engineering, a tactic that exploits human psychology, is another facet of cyber threats. Picture a skilled manipulator who convinces individuals to divulge confidential information willingly. This psychological ploy is often more challenging to guard against, as it preys on human trust and emotions.

Ransomware, a particularly insidious threat, encrypts a user's files, demanding payment for their release. It's like a digital hostage situation where the victim must choose between losing valuable data and succumbing to the demands of the cyber kidnapper. The consequences of such attacks extend beyond financial losses to erode trust in digital systems.

In this dynamic landscape, the threats are not static; they evolve and adapt. What might seem like a secure fortress today could become a vulnerable target tomorrow. Understanding these threats is not only a necessity but an ongoing process. It requires a vigilant mindset, akin to navigating a constantly changing maze where adaptability and proactive measures are crucial. As we continue to rely on digital technology for every facet of our lives, comprehending these threats becomes imperative in safeguarding our digital homes from the ever-present shadows that lurk in the virtual realm.

Navigating the realm of cybersecurity involves unraveling a tapestry of concepts and terminology, akin to deciphering a complex language that safeguards our digital existence. At its essence, cybersecurity is the practice of defending computer systems, networks, and data from unauthorized access, attacks, and damage. It's the digital guardian that stands between our virtual world and the myriad threats that seek to exploit vulnerabilities. One fundamental concept is encryption, a process that transforms data into an unreadable format, accessible only to those with the appropriate decryption key. It's like encoding a secret message that can only be decoded by someone with the right cipher.

Firewalls, another cornerstone, act as virtual barriers between a trusted internal network and untrusted external networks, controlling the flow of traffic and preventing unauthorized access. Picture it as a security checkpoint that filters out potential threats before they can breach the digital borders. Antivirus software, a familiar term in the cybersecurity lexicon, is akin to a vigilant sentinel scanning for and removing malicious software, much like a virtual immune system defending against digital infections.

Two-factor authentication (2FA) adds an extra layer of security by requiring users to provide two different forms of identification before accessing a system. Think of it as having both a key and a fingerprint to unlock a door, ensuring that even if one factor is compromised, there's an additional barrier to entry. Intrusion Detection Systems (IDS) and Intrusion Prevention Systems (IPS) are cybersecurity tools that monitor network and/or system activities for malicious actions or policy violations. They serve as virtual watchdogs, alerting administrators to potential threats and, in the case of IPS, actively preventing unauthorized access.

The concept of "zero trust" has gained prominence in recent years, challenging the traditional notion of trusting entities within a network. In a zero-trust model, no entity, whether inside or outside the network, is trusted by default. Verification is required from everyone, adding an extra layer of caution in an era where threats can emerge from within as well as outside the traditional security perimeters.

As our digital landscape expands, the Internet of Things (IoT) introduces a host of new concepts. IoT refers to the network of interconnected devices that communicate and share data. While offering convenience, these devices also pose security challenges, as each connected device becomes a potential entry point for cyber threats.

Understanding these cybersecurity concepts and terminology is akin to acquiring a new language, one that empowers individuals and organizations to navigate the digital realm with confidence. In a world where technology evolves rapidly, staying fluent in this language is not just an option but a necessity for fortifying our digital defenses against the ever-adapting landscape of cyber threats.

In the intricate tapestry of our digital age, the imperative for cybersecurity transcends mere technicality; it is a safeguard for the very essence of our modern existence. Picture the digital landscape as a bustling city, with every click, transaction, and interaction representing a step into its dynamic streets. Now, consider the vast array of information traversing these virtual avenues – personal data, financial details, intellectual property, all woven into the fabric of our interconnected lives. The need for cybersecurity arises as a response to the inherent vulnerability of this intricate web, where the convergence of personal, corporate, and governmental interests creates a landscape ripe for exploitation.

At the heart of this imperative lies the protection of sensitive information. In an era where our lives are intricately woven into the digital fabric, from online banking to social media interactions, the stakes have never been higher. Cybersecurity becomes the digital shield that guards the gates to our private domains, preventing unauthorized access and ensuring the confidentiality of our personal and financial data. It's akin to securing the doors and windows of our homes, ensuring that only trusted individuals have access to our most intimate spaces.

Beyond personal security, the economic landscape is increasingly reliant on digital infrastructure. Consider the vast networks that underpin global commerce, where financial transactions, supply chains, and critical infrastructure are interconnected. Cybersecurity becomes the guardian of economic stability, preventing digital marauders from disrupting the seamless flow of commerce. Just as medieval fortresses protected cities from external threats, cybersecurity fortifies the economic foundations of our interconnected world.

In the realm of intellectual property and innovation, the need for cybersecurity becomes even more pronounced. Corporations invest substantial resources in research and development, creating a digital repository of proprietary information. Cyber threats, ranging from industrial espionage to Ransomware attacks, pose a direct threat to these intellectual assets. The protection of innovation, trade secrets, and proprietary data becomes a paramount concern, and cybersecurity emerges as the custodian of these digital treasures.

In the broader context of national security, the interconnectedness of digital networks has profound implications. Governments store sensitive information related to defense, intelligence, and critical infrastructure in digital repositories. A breach in these systems could compromise not only national secrets but also the very infrastructure that sustains the functioning of a nation. Cybersecurity becomes a linchpin in the defense against digital threats, ensuring the sovereignty and security of nations in the face of an ever-evolving cyber landscape.

Moreover, as our lives become increasingly intertwined with smart technologies and the Internet of Things (IoT), the attack surface for cyber threats expands exponentially. From smart homes to autonomous vehicles, the need for cybersecurity extends beyond traditional computing devices. It becomes the guardian of our interconnected future, where the vulnerabilities of one device can have cascading effects on the entire network.

In summary, the need for effective cybersecurity is not just a technological necessity; it is a fundamental component of our collective well-being in the digital era. It safeguards our privacy, protects our economic foundations, preserves our intellectual capital, and secures the very fabric of our nations. As we navigate the ever-evolving digital landscape, the imperative for robust cybersecurity measures becomes not just a choice but an ethical and societal responsibility, ensuring that the promise of our interconnected world is not overshadowed by the shadows of digital threats.

Chapter 1

NETWORK SECURITY

UNDERSTANDING THE BASICS OF NETWORK SECURITY

Network security serves as a critical safeguard and ensures the protection of valuable information within the complex web of digital communication pathways. There are many key components that make up this concept.

Access Control

At the heart of network security lies the concept of access control, a mechanism that regulates entry to the network based on user credentials and permissions. Similar to a vigilant bouncer at a club entrance, access control ensures that only authorized individuals or devices can access specific resources within the network. This not only safeguards sensitive information but also prevents potential disruptions or unauthorized data extraction.

Encryption

Encryption, a fundamental pillar of network security, acts as the secret language of the digital realm. This process transforms data into an unreadable format, accessible only to those with the appropriate decryption key. Analogous to encoding a message for a specific recipient, encryption guarantees that even if an unauthorized entity gains access to the network, intercepted data remains indecipherable and secure.

Firewalls

In the metaphorical cityscape of the digital world, firewalls stand as digital guardians at the gateway of a network. These vigilant security checkpoints monitor and control incoming and outgoing traffic, filtering data based on predetermined security rules. By doing so, firewalls prevent unauthorized access and protect against a spectrum of cyber threats, playing a crucial role in the defense mechanisms of the digital city.

Intrusion Detection Systems (IDS) and Intrusion Prevention Systems (IPS)

Intrusion Detection Systems (IDS) and Intrusion Prevention Systems (IPS) act as watchful sentinels, constantly monitoring network activities for unusual patterns or suspicious behavior. When potential threats are detected, an IDS raises an alert, while an IPS takes proactive measures to prevent or block identified threats. These systems serve as the watchful eyes that scan the digital streets for signs of trouble, ensuring a swift and proactive response to potential security breaches.

Principle of Least Privilege: Minimizing Risks

The principle of least privilege is a foundational philosophy in network security. This principle advocates for providing users or systems with only the minimum level of access necessary to perform their tasks. Analogous to distributing keys to various rooms in a building, each user receives only the keys they need. This minimizes the risk of unauthorized access and potential breaches, reinforcing the overall security posture of the network.

The regular application of security patches and updates serves as the immune system of the digital realm. Just as the human body requires vaccinations and updates to defend against new threats, networks must undergo continuous maintenance to address vulnerabilities and enhance resilience against emerging cyber risks. This proactive approach strengthens the network's ability to withstand evolving security challenges.

In essence, comprehending the basics of network security involves navigating through these fundamental principles, each contributing to the construction of a robust and resilient defense system in our interconnected digital city.

FIREWALLS, INTRUSION DETECTION AND PREVENTION SYSTEMS

Firewalls

In the expansive landscape of digital communication, firewalls emerge as stalwart guardians, stationed at the gateway of networks to protect against a multitude of cyber threats. Imagine them as vigilant sentinels, scrutinizing each piece of data attempting to traverse the network's boundaries. In essence, firewalls are the digital checkpoints that monitor and control incoming and outgoing traffic, playing a crucial role in the defense mechanisms of our interconnected world.

At its core, a firewall is a barrier designed to prevent unauthorized access to or from a private network while allowing legitimate communication to flow freely. It operates based on a set of predetermined security rules, akin to a city gatekeeper who allows only those with the proper credentials to enter. These security rules dictate which data packets are allowed or denied access, effectively establishing a line of defense against potential cyber threats.

Firewalls come in various forms, with each type serving specific purposes within the realm of network security. The traditional packet-filtering firewall examines data packets and makes decisions based on factors such as source and destination addresses, ports, and protocols. Think of it as a meticulous customs agent inspecting each item entering or leaving the country, determining whether it meets the predefined criteria for passage.

Stateful inspection firewalls, on the other hand, take a more sophisticated approach. They not only consider individual data packets but also assess the state of the connection. This means they have an awareness of the context of the communication, allowing them to make more informed decisions about whether to permit or block specific data streams. It's akin to a gatekeeper not only inspecting individual items but also considering the ongoing conversation between individuals.

Proxy firewalls act as intermediaries between internal and external systems, intercepting requests from clients and forwarding them to the destination. This intermediary role adds an extra layer of security, as the internal network is shielded behind the proxy, preventing direct access. Picture it as a secretary receiving and vetting requests before allowing them to reach the intended recipient, ensuring that only legitimate and safe requests pass through.

Firewalls are not static entities; they evolve to meet the demands of an ever-changing cybersecurity landscape. Next- generation firewalls, for instance, combine traditional firewall capabilities with advanced features like intrusion prevention, application awareness, and deep packet inspection. These sophisticated guardians go beyond simple access control, offering a comprehensive defense against modern cyber threats.

In a world where the digital realm is both expansive and interconnected, firewalls play a crucial role in securing the gateways to our virtual cities. They stand as the first line of defense, diligently monitoring and filtering the vast stream of data flowing through the digital highways, ensuring that only authorized and secure communication traverses the network's boundaries.

Intrusion Detection Systems (IDS)

Within a network, Intrusion Detection Systems (IDS) emerge as watchful eyes, tirelessly scanning for signs of potential threats and anomalies. Imagine them as vigilant sentinels patrolling the digital streets, attuned to the subtle cues that may indicate an impending security breach. IDS plays a pivotal role in network security by detecting and alerting unusual patterns or activities that deviate from the norm.

The primary function of an IDS is to monitor network and/or system activities in real-time, analyzing data for any indications of unauthorized access, security policy violations, or abnormal behavior. It's akin to a security camera surveying a busy street, triggering an alarm if it detects any suspicious activity. IDS operates on the principle of anomaly detection, identifying deviations from established baselines that may signify a potential security threat.

There are two main types of IDS: network-based and host-based. Network-based IDS examines network traffic for suspicious patterns, focusing on the data flowing through the network.

Host-based IDS, on the other hand, monitors the activities on individual devices or hosts within the network, looking for signs of compromise or malicious behavior. Together, these two types provide a comprehensive surveillance system, covering both the broader network landscape and the specific devices within it.

When an IDS identifies a potential threat, it generates an alert to notify administrators or security personnel. This alert serves as an early warning system, allowing for a swift and targeted response to mitigate the potential impact of the threat. Picture it as a neighborhood watch, where vigilant residents alert each other to any unusual activities, enabling a collective effort to maintain the security of the community.

Intrusion Detection Systems can operate in a passive or active mode. In passive mode, the IDS monitors and alerts but does not take direct action against the detected threats. Active mode, on the other hand, involves the IDS taking proactive measures to prevent or block the identified threats. The choice between passive and active modes depends on the specific security requirements and risk tolerance of the network.

Continuous refinement is crucial for the effectiveness of IDS. Regular updates to threat signatures, which are patterns or indicators of known threats, ensure that the system remains vigilant against the latest cyber threats. Additionally, tuning the IDS to the specific characteristics of the network helps reduce false positives and negatives, enhancing the accuracy of threat detection.

In summary, Intrusion Detection Systems serve as the watchful eyes that tirelessly scan the digital landscape for signs of trouble. By detecting and alerting to potential threats in real-time, IDS plays a crucial role in maintaining the security and integrity of the network, contributing to the overall resilience of our inter-connected digital communities.

Intrusion Prevention Systems (IPS)

In cybersecurity, Intrusion Prevention Systems (IPS) emerge as proactive defenders, going beyond the watchful eyes of Intrusion Detection Systems to actively prevent and mitigate potential threats. Imagine them as digital sentinels equipped not only with the ability to detect signs of trouble but also with the power to intervene and thwart malicious activities before they can inflict harm.

While Intrusion Detection Systems focus on identifying and alerting to potential threats, Intrusion Prevention Systems take a step further by actively blocking or mitigating those threats in real-time. It's akin to a security guard not only spotting a suspicious individual but also intervening to prevent any potential harm. IPS operates on the principle of immediate response, leveraging both signature-based and anomaly-based detection methods to identify and neutralize threats.

One of the primary functions of an IPS is to examine network and/or system activities for patterns that match known signatures of cyber threats. These signatures, akin to fingerprints of known criminals, allow the IPS to swiftly identify and block activities associated with specific malicious entities or activities. Additionally, anomaly-based detection methods analyze deviations from established baselines, enabling the IPS to identify and prevent previously unknown threats.

IPS operates in-line with network traffic, allowing it to actively intervene and block potentially malicious activities in real-time.

This proactive approach is particularly valuable in preventing threats that may exploit vulnerabilities before they can manifest as a full-scale attack. Think of it as a digital immune system, ready to respond to the slightest signs of a potential infection to ensure the overall health and integrity of the network.

Similar to Intrusion Detection Systems, IPS can operate in passive or active mode. In passive mode, the system monitors and alerts but does not actively intervene. Active mode involves the IPS taking immediate action to prevent or block the identified threats. The choice between passive and active modes depends on the specific security requirements and risk tolerance of the network.

The ability to respond to evolving threats is a cornerstone of IPS effectiveness. Regular updates to threat signatures, much like updating a vaccine to protect against new strains of a virus, ensure that the system remains equipped to identify and prevent the latest cyber threats. Additionally, continuous refinement and tuning based on the specific characteristics of the network enhance the accuracy and efficacy of IPS in safeguarding the digital landscape.

Intrusion Prevention Systems, with their proactive defense mechanisms, play a crucial role in the resilience of network security. By actively preventing and mitigating potential threats in real-time, IPS contributes to the overall strength and integrity of our interconnected digital communities, providing a robust line of defense against the dynamic landscape of cyber threats.

SECURING WIRELESS NETWORKS

In our digitally-driven world, where the seamless flow of information is paramount, securing wireless networks becomes a critical imperative. Wireless networks have become ubiquitous, providing the flexibility and convenience of connectivity without the constraints of physical cables. However, this convenience comes with its own set of challenges, as wireless networks are susceptible to a range of security threats. To build a fortified digital haven, one must navigate through the intricate landscape of wireless network security, understanding the vulnerabilities and implementing robust measures to safeguard against potential risks.

Understanding Wireless Networks

Wireless networks, often referred to as Wi-Fi networks, enable devices to connect and communicate without the need for physical cables. This freedom of mobility has revolutionized the way we access information, from the comfort of our homes to bustling coffee shops and corporate offices. However, the very openness that defines wireless networks also exposes them to potential security threats. Understanding the intricacies of these networks is the first step in fortifying their defenses.

Wireless networks operate by transmitting data over radio waves, allowing devices equipped with wireless network adapters to connect to access points (APs) that serve as the entry points to the network. These access points are the digital gateways, facilitating communication between devices and the broader network or the internet. The challenge lies in securing this wireless communication channel, ensuring that only authorized devices gain access while preventing malicious entities from exploiting vulnerabilities.

The Key Players in Wireless Network Security

Securing wireless networks involves understanding the key players in the security landscape and implementing measures to mitigate potential risks. Let's explore these key components:

Wireless Routers and Access Points

Wireless routers and access points are the central components of a wireless network, serving as the gatekeepers that control access and facilitate communication. Securing these devices is crucial, as they define the entry points to the network. This involves changing default passwords, regularly updating firmware, and configuring security settings such as encryption protocols and network names (SSID).

Wireless Encryption

Encryption is the process of encoding data to make it unreadable without the appropriate decryption key. In the context of wireless networks, securing the data transmitted between devices and access points is paramount. Wi-Fi Protected Access (WPA) and its successor WPA2/WPA3 are encryption protocols commonly used to safeguard wireless communications. Employing strong encryption ensures that even if unauthorized entities intercept the data, they cannot decipher its contents without the encryption key.

Network Authentication

Authentication mechanisms are crucial in ensuring that only authorized devices gain access to the wireless network. Wi-Fi networks typically use pre-shared keys (PSK) or more robust methods like Extensible Authentication Protocol (EAP) for authentication. Complex passwords and the use of strong authentication protocols contribute to the overall resilience of the network against unauthorized access.

Wireless Intrusion Detection and Prevention Systems (WIDS/WIPS)

Wireless Intrusion Detection Systems (WIDS) and Wireless Intrusion Prevention Systems (WIPS) act as vigilant guards, monitoring wireless networks for signs of unauthorized access or suspicious activities. WIDS detects potential threats and anomalies, while WIPS takes proactive measures to prevent or mitigate identified threats. These systems provide an additional layer of defense against evolving security risks.

Common Threats to Wireless Networks

Understanding the common threats to wireless networks is essential for devising effective security strategies. Let's explore some of the shadows that lurk in the digital realm:

Eavesdropping

Eavesdropping involves unauthorized individuals intercepting and monitoring wireless communications. Without encryption, data transmitted over the airwaves is susceptible to eavesdropping. Employing robust encryption protocols, such as WPA3, mitigates the risk of eavesdropping by ensuring that intercepted data remains indecipherable.

Unauthorized Access

Unauthorized access occurs when malicious entities gain entry to a wireless network without proper authentication. This can lead to unauthorized use of network resources or potential data breaches. Implementing strong authentication mechanisms, regularly updating passwords, and employing intrusion detection systems help thwart unauthorized access attempts.

Man-in-the-Middle (Met) Attacks

In a Man-in-the-Middle attack, an intruder intercepts and potentially alters the communication between two parties without their knowledge. This can lead to the compromise of sensitive information. Encryption, coupled with techniques like certificate-based authentication, helps safeguard against Met attacks by ensuring the integrity and confidentiality of wireless communications.

Rogue Access Points

Rogue access points are unauthorized wireless access points that are set up without the knowledge or consent of network administrators. These can pose serious security risks by providing an entry point for attackers or creating opportunities for eavesdropping. Regularly scanning for and identifying rogue access points, coupled with strong access controls, mitigates this threat.

Building a Fortified Wireless Network: Best Practices

Fortifying wireless networks requires a multifaceted approach that encompasses both technical measures and user awareness. Here are some best practices for building a secure wireless network:

Change Default Credentials

Changing default usernames and passwords for wireless routers and access points is a fundamental step in securing the network. Default credentials are well-known to attackers, and changing them ensures that unauthorized entities cannot easily gain access to network devices.

Implement Strong Encryption

Choosing and implementing strong encryption protocols, such as WPA3, ensures that data transmitted over the wireless network remains confidential and secure. Strong encryption is a foundational element in building a resilient defense against eavesdropping and unauthorized access.

Use Complex Passwords and Authentication Protocols

Employing complex passwords and robust authentication protocols adds an additional layer of defense against unauthorized access. Strong authentication mechanisms, such as WPA3's Simultaneous Authentication of Equals (SAE), contribute to the overall security of the wireless network.

Regularly Update Firmware

Firmware updates provided by device manufacturers often include security patches and enhancements. Regularly updating the firmware for wireless routers and access points ensures that known vulnerabilities are addressed, strengthening the overall security posture of the network.

Enable Network Segmentation

Segmenting the wireless network into separate virtual LANs (VLANs) adds an extra layer of security by isolating different types of traffic. This prevents unauthorized access to sensitive areas of the network and limits the potential impact of security breaches.

Monitor for Rogue Access Points

Regularly scanning for and identifying rogue access points helps detect unauthorized devices that may pose security risks. This proactive approach allows network administrators to take swift action to mitigate potential threats and maintain control over the network's integrity.

Educate Users

User awareness is a critical component of wireless network security. Educating users about the risks of connecting to unsecured networks, the importance of strong passwords, and the need for vigilance against phishing attempts enhances the overall security posture of the network.

Implement Wireless Intrusion Detection and Prevention Systems

Deploying Wireless Intrusion Detection Systems (WIDS) and Wireless Intrusion Prevention Systems (WIPS) adds an extra layer of defense against potential threats. These systems actively monitor and respond to suspicious activities, contributing to the overall resilience of the wireless network.

Regular Security Audits

Conducting regular security audits helps identify and address potential vulnerabilities in the wireless network. This ongoing assessment ensures that the network's defenses are aligned with evolving security requirements and best practices.

Guest Network Isolation

If the wireless network includes a guest network for visitors, isolating it from the internal network adds an additional layer of security. This prevents potential threats originating from guest devices from affecting the core infrastructure.

Chapter 2

MALWARE AND ANTIVIRUS

UNDERSTANDING MALWARE

In the vast and interconnected landscape of the digital world, the term "malware" looms ominously, embodying a shadowy threat that can infiltrate, disrupt, and compromise the very essence of our digital existence. Understanding malware requires delving into the intricate realm of malicious software, exploring its forms, functions, and the profound impact it can have on individuals, organizations, and even societies. As we embark on this journey, we'll unravel the enigma of malware in human-like style, shedding light on its complexities and the crucial role of antivirus solutions in safeguarding our digital realms.

Malware Unveiled

At its core, "malware" is a portmanteau of "malicious software," encompassing a diverse array of code crafted with nefarious intent. Imagine malware as a digital intruder, stealthily breaching the walls of your computer or network, often with the goal of extracting sensitive information, disrupting operations, or exerting control for malicious purposes.

Forms of Malware

The world of malware is vast and varied, with different forms of malicious software engineered to exploit vulnerabilities and achieve distinct objectives. Let's explore some of the prominent members of the digital rogues' gallery:

Viruses

Viruses are akin to digital contagions, capable of attaching themselves to legitimate programs and spreading from one host to another. Once activated, they can execute malicious code, replicate, and potentially corrupt or delete files. The insidious nature of viruses lies in their ability to hide within seemingly harmless software, waiting for an opportunity to strike.

Worms

Worms are self-replicating malware that can spread across networks without requiring user interaction. Unlike viruses, worms can operate independently, exploiting vulnerabilities to propagate and infect multiple systems. Their capacity for autonomous spread makes them particularly potent in the digital landscape.

Trojans

Named after the classical story of the Trojan horse, Trojan malware disguises itself as legitimate software or files, deceiving users into unknowingly installing malicious code. Once inside, Trojans can carry out a range of malicious activities, from stealing sensitive information to creating backdoors for remote access.

Ransomware

Ransomware encrypts a user's files and demands a ransom in exchange for the decryption key. It's like a digital kidnapper, holding your data hostage until you meet its demands. The impact of Ransomware can be devastating, with the potential to cripple businesses, institutions, and even individual users.

Spyware

Spyware operates stealthily, collecting information about a user's activities without their knowledge or consent. It can monitor keystrokes, capture screenshots, and track online behavior. The insidious nature of spyware lies in its ability to silently survey, potentially exposing sensitive and private information.

Adware

While not as malicious as other forms of malware, adware bombards users with unwanted advertisements, often leading to a degraded user experience. It may also track user behavior to deliver targeted ads. Though less harmful, adware can be intrusive and undermine the overall integrity of a user's digital environment.

Botnets

Botnets are networks of compromised computers, often controlled by a central command (bot herder). These armies of infected machines, known as bots, can be harnessed for various malicious activities, such as launching Distributed Denial-Of-Service (DDoS) attacks or spreading spam. The collective power of a botnet amplifies the impact of cyberattacks.

Propagation and Infection: The Digital Plague

Understanding how malware spreads and infects systems is akin to deciphering the mechanisms of a digital plague. Malicious software employs various tactics to infiltrate its targets, exploiting vulnerabilities in software, social engineering, or a combination of both.

Exploiting Vulnerabilities

Malware often takes advantage of vulnerabilities in software or operating systems. These vulnerabilities may be unintentional flaws that software developers hadn't anticipated. Once identified, cybercriminals craft malware to exploit these weaknesses, infiltrating systems and leaving a trail of compromise in their wake.

Social Engineering

Social engineering involves manipulating individuals into divulging confidential information or performing actions that compromise security. Malware creators may employ tactics like phishing emails, fraudulent websites, or deceptive messages to trick users into downloading and executing malicious code. The human factor becomes the unwitting accomplice in the propagation of malware.

Drive-by Downloads

Drive-by downloads occur when malware is automatically downloaded onto a user's device without their knowledge or consent. This often happens when visiting compromised websites or clicking on malicious ads. The user becomes an unwitting victim, with the malware silently establishing its presence in the background.

The Impact of Malware: Digital Consequences

The consequences of a malware infection can be profound, extending beyond the digital realm to impact individuals, businesses, and even the fabric of society. Let's explore the multifaceted impact of malware:

Data Breaches

Malware, particularly those designed for data theft, can lead to severe privacy breaches. Personal and sensitive information, ranging from financial details to login credentials, can be infiltrated and misused. The aftermath of a data breach often involves legal repercussions, financial losses, and reputational damage.

Financial Losses

For businesses, the financial losses resulting from a malware attack can be staggering. Ransomware attacks, in particular, can cripple operations, leading to downtime, loss of revenue, and the potential payment of hefty ransoms. The economic impact of malware extends beyond individual victims to affect the broader economic landscape.

Disruption of Operations

Malware has the power to disrupt critical operations within organizations. Whether through the destruction of files, encryption of data, or interference with network functions, the consequences can be severe. Operational disruptions can lead to a loss of productivity, damage to business continuity, and the need for extensive recovery efforts.

Compromised Security

Malware compromises the security posture of systems and networks. This breach can extend beyond the infected device to impact interconnected systems, creating a domino effect of vulnerabilities. The compromised security may lead to further attacks, exposing a widening attack surface for cybercriminals.

Loss of Trust

The psychological impact of malware is often underestimated. Beyond the tangible losses, the erosion of trust is a profound consequence. Individuals may become wary of online activities, businesses may struggle to regain customer confidence, and the fabric of digital trust may be frayed.

Antivirus Solutions: Digital Guardians

In the face of this digital threat landscape, antivirus solutions emerge as digital guardians, standing as a last line of defense against the encroaching tide of malware.

Understanding how antivirus software operates involves grasping its functions, methodologies, and the ongoing cat- and-mouse game between cybersecurity defenders and cybercriminals.

Signature-Based Detection

Signature-based detection is akin to recognizing digital finger-prints. Antivirus software maintains a database of known malware signatures – unique patterns or characteristics associated with specific malicious code. When the antivirus scans a file, it compares its digital fingerprint against the signatures in its database. If a match is found, the file is flagged as potentially malicious.

Heuristic-Based Detection

Heuristic-based detection operates on the principle of digital intuition. Instead of relying solely on known signatures, the antivirus uses heuristic analysis to identify potentially suspicious behavior. This approach is proactive, allowing the software to detect previously unknown malware based on its behavior or characteristics that deviate from the norm.

Behavioral Analysis

Behavioral analysis involves monitoring the behavior of software in real-time. Antivirus solutions scrutinize how a program or file behaves when executed, identifying actions indicative of malicious intent. This dynamic approach enhances the ability to detect malware that may exhibit different behaviors over time or employ evasion techniques to bypass traditional detection methods.

Sandboxing

Sandboxing involves isolating potentially malicious files in a controlled environment called a sandbox. This allows the antivirus software to execute the file and observe its behavior without risking harm to the actual system. If the file exhibits malicious behavior, it is flagged and prevented from affecting the real system.

Cloud-Based Detection

Cloud-based detection leverages the collective intelligence of a vast network of interconnected devices. When an antivirus solution encounters a potential threat, it can query a cloud-based database to determine whether the file or code is recognized as malicious by other users. This real-time sharing of threat intelligence enhances the antivirus software's ability to respond to emerging threats.

The Cat-and-Mouse Game: Digital Evolution

The relationship between antivirus solutions and malware creators is a perpetual cat-and-mouse game. As antivirus software evolves to detect and mitigate new threats, cybercriminals respond by devising innovative techniques to bypass defenses. This dynamic interplay underscores the need for continuous updates, adaptive strategies, and a proactive approach to cybersecurity.

Evolution of Malware

Malware creators constantly refine their techniques to evade detection. They may employ polymorphic or metamorphic methods, changing the appearance of their code with each iteration to create unique instances that are challenging for traditional signature-based detection to identify. The ability of malware to evolve necessitates a similarly adaptive response from antivirus solutions.

Zero-Day Exploits

Zero-day exploits target vulnerabilities that are unknown to software developers or security vendors. Cybercriminals capitalize on these undisclosed weaknesses to launch attacks that can bypass traditional security measures. Antivirus solutions must employ advanced detection methods, such as heuristic analysis and behavioral monitoring, to detect and mitigate zero-day threats.

Advanced Persistent Threats (APTs)

APTs are sophisticated and prolonged cyberattacks that often involve targeted and stealthy infiltration. These attacks may use a combination of malware, social engineering, and persistent efforts to remain undetected within a network. Defending against APTs requires a multi- layered security approach, combining antivirus solutions with intrusion detection systems and proactive threat hunting.

Best Practices for Malware Defense: Digital Vigilance

Understanding malware and the role of antivirus solutions is foundational, but effective defense requires a holistic approach. Here are best practices for individuals and organizations to enhance their malware defenses:

Keep Software Updated

Regularly updating software and operating systems is a fundamental defense against malware. Updates often include security patches that address known vulnerabilities, reducing the risk of exploitation by cybercriminals.

Use Strong, Unique Passwords

Employing strong and unique passwords for online accounts adds an additional layer of defense. This practice prevents unauthorized access even if one account is compromised, reducing the potential impact of a security breach.

Exercise Caution with Email

Phishing emails remain a prevalent vector for malware distribution. Exercise caution with email attachments and links, especially if they come from unknown or suspicious sources. Verify the legitimacy of emails before interacting with their content.

Implement Network Security Measures

Network security measures, such as firewalls and intrusion detection/prevention systems, provide a fortified perimeter against malware. These measures can help identify and block malicious activities before they reach individual devices.

Backup Critical Data

Regularly backing up critical data is a prudent practice. In the event of a malware infection, having recent backups ensures that data can be restored, mitigating the impact of data loss or Ransomware attacks.

TYPES OF MALWARE AND THEIR CHARACTERISTICS

Understanding the diverse types of malware is paramount in navigating the ever-evolving landscape of cybersecurity. Picture this landscape as a digital ecosystem, with each type of malware representing a distinct species with its own behaviors, methods of infection, and potential impacts on computer systems and networks.

Viruses

Viruses are akin to the pathogens of the digital world. They attach themselves to legitimate programs or files, effectively "infecting" them. Once a user executes the infected program or file, the virus gains access to the system and replicates itself, spreading to other files and potentially other systems. Viruses can be designed to deliver payloads that range from simply annoying pop-ups to destructive actions that can harm files or compromise system integrity.

Characteristics
- Infection Mechanism: Requires user interaction to execute the infected file.
- Spread: Can spread through infected files or programs, often relying on human behavior to propagate.
- Payloads: May have varying payloads, from harmless pranks to serious damage.

Worms

Worms are relentless travelers in the digital ecosystem, exploiting vulnerabilities to spread across networks and systems. Unlike viruses, worms can operate independently, not relying on user interaction to propagate. They exploit weaknesses in network security, rapidly spreading from one system to another. Worms can have a wide range of payloads, from simply replicating themselves to carrying out more malicious actions.

Characteristics
- Infection Mechanism: Exploits vulnerabilities to spread autonomously, without requiring user interaction.
- Spread: Can move across networks, infecting multiple systems.
- Payloads: May carry a variety of payloads, including data theft, system disruption, or facilitating other forms of malware.

Trojans

Trojans, named after the legendary Greek horse, are deceptive pieces of software that masquerade as legitimate and desirable programs. Users unwittingly download and install Trojans, often thinking they are harmless or beneficial applications. Once inside a system, Trojans open a backdoor, allowing cybercriminals unauthorized access. They can be used to steal sensitive information, launch attacks, or facilitate the installation of other malware.

Characteristics
- Disguise: Pretends to be a legitimate program to deceive users.
- Infection Mechanism: Relies on user deception to gain access to systems.
- Payloads: Can facilitate various malicious activities, including data theft, system manipulation, or acting as a backdoor for other malware.

Ransomware

Ransomware has gained notoriety as a particularly insidious form of malware. Its primary objective is to encrypt files on a victim's system, rendering them inaccessible. The cybercriminal then demands a ransom – usually in crypto currency – in exchange for the decryption key. Ransomware often spreads through phishing emails or malicious downloads. The impact can be severe, with individuals, businesses, and even governmental organizations falling victim to these digital extortionists.

Characteristics
- Encryption: Encrypts files to make them inaccessible.
- Ransom Demand: Typically demands payment in crypto currency for the decryption key.

- Spread: Often relies on social engineering tactics, phishing, or exploiting software vulnerabilities.

Spyware

Spyware is designed to discreetly observe and collect information about a user's online activities without their knowledge or consent. It can capture keystrokes, record browsing habits, and even take screenshots. The harvested information is then sent to the malware creator, who may use it for various purposes, including identity theft, espionage, or targeted advertising.

Characteristics
- Covert Observation: Monitors user activities without their awareness.
- Information Collection: Captures sensitive information for malicious purposes.
- Payloads: May facilitate identity theft, financial fraud, or unauthorized surveillance.

Adware

While adware may not be as malicious as other forms of malware, it can still be a nuisance and compromise user experience. Adware bombards users with unwanted advertisements, often leading to a degradation of system performance. Adware may come bundled with seemingly legitimate software, and its primary purpose is to generate revenue for the creators through clicks on ads.

Characteristics
- Unwanted Advertisements: Displays intrusive and often irrelevant ads.
- System Impact: Can slow down system performance and

compromise user experience.
- Revenue Generation: Generates income for creators through ad clicks.

Botnets

Botnets are networks of compromised computers, often referred to as "bots" or "zombies," controlled by a central command and control server. These digital armies can be used to carry out coordinated attacks, such as Distributed Denial of Service (DDoS) attacks, or to facilitate other malicious activities like spamming or data theft. The compromise of individual computers within a botnet is often the result of other malware, such as worms or Trojans.

Characteristics
- Controlled Network: Compromised computers are remotely controlled by a central server.
- Coordinated Attacks: Can be used to carry out coordinated cyber-attacks.
- Multipurpose: Often employed for various malicious activities, depending on the goals of the botnet creator.

Rootkits

Rootkits are a form of malware designed to conceal their presence on a system, making them particularly difficult to detect. Once installed, rootkits provide unauthorized access to a system and can manipulate or replace system functions, enabling other malware to persist undetected. Rootkits often exploit vulnerabilities in the operating system to gain privileged access.

Characteristics
- Stealth: Conceals its presence and activities to evade detection.
- Privileged Access: Exploits vulnerabilities to gain elevated system privileges.
- Persistence: Facilitates the long-term presence of other malware on a compromised system.

Evolution of Malware and Defense Strategies

The landscape of malware is dynamic and continually evolving as cybercriminals adapt to advancements in technology and security measures. To counter these threats, cybersecurity professionals employ a combination of proactive and reactive defense strategies.

Proactive Defense

Proactive defense involves implementing measures to prevent malware infections before they occur. This includes:

Firewalls and Intrusion Prevention Systems (IPS)

Act as digital gatekeepers, monitoring and controlling network traffic to prevent unauthorized access and the spread of malware.

Security Awareness Training

Educates users about potential threats, emphasizing safe online practices to reduce the likelihood of falling victim to social engineering tactics.

Regular Software Updates and Patch Management

Ensures that systems are equipped with the latest security patches, closing potential vulnerabilities that malware may exploit.

Network Segmentation

Divides networks into segments to contain the spread of malware in the event of a breach, limiting its impact.

Reactive Defense

Reactive defense focuses on detecting and mitigating malware infections after they have occurred. Key components include:

Antivirus and Anti-malware Software

Scans and detects malicious files or activities on a system, removing or quarantining them to prevent further harm.

Incident Response Plans

Outlines procedures for responding to and containing malware incidents, minimizing the impact on systems and data.

Data Backups

Regularly backs up critical data to facilitate recovery in the event of a Ransomware attack or other data loss incidents.

Digital Forensics

Investigates and analyzes malware incidents to understand their origins, methods, and potential impacts, aiding in the development of stronger defense strategies.

ANTIVIRUS SOFTWARE

Imagine antivirus software as a vigilant guardian, standing watch over the digital realms of our devices, tirelessly scanning, detecting, and neutralizing malicious entities that seek to compromise our security and privacy.

The Digital Guardian: What is Antivirus Software?

At its core, antivirus software is a digital shield designed to protect our computers, laptops, smartphones, and other devices from malicious software, commonly known as malware. Malware encompasses a broad spectrum of digital threats, including viruses, worms, Trojans, Ransomware, and more. Antivirus software serves as a formidable defense mechanism, continuously evolving to keep pace with the ever-changing tactics of cybercriminals.

How does it Work?

Understanding the functionality of antivirus software is akin to unraveling the tactics of a digital detective. Here are the key components of its arsenal:

Signature-Based Detection

One of the foundational methods employed by antivirus software is signature-based detection. It involves the creation and maintenance of a database of digital "signatures" or fingerprints that represent known malware. These signatures are unique identifiers that help the antivirus software recognize and block malicious files or patterns. When a user initiates a scan, the antivirus compares the files on the device against its signature database, identifying and isolating any matches.

Heuristic-Based Detection

Heuristic-based detection is a more advanced approach that goes beyond relying solely on known signatures. Antivirus software using heuristic analysis examines the behavior of programs and files, looking for patterns or characteristics that may indicate malicious intent. This proactive approach enables the software to detect previously unknown or "zero-day" threats that lack a known signature. It's like a detective anticipating the moves of a criminal based on behavioral patterns.

Behavioral-Based Detection

Behavioral-based detection takes the analysis a step further by monitoring the behavior of programs and files in real-time. Instead of relying solely on predefined signatures or predicted patterns, this method observes how software behaves once it is executed. If a program exhibits suspicious or malicious behavior, such as attempting to modify system files or replicate itself, the antivirus software can intervene to prevent further damage.

Sandboxing

Sandboxing involves isolating suspicious files in a virtual environment, commonly referred to as a "sandbox." This controlled space allows the antivirus software to execute and analyze the file's behavior without risking harm to the actual system. If the file is deemed malicious, it can be contained within the sandbox, preventing it from affecting the rest of the device. It's analogous to placing a potentially hazardous substance in a sealed laboratory for analysis.

Cloud-Based Detection

Cloud-based detection leverages the power of collective intelligence and real-time updates. Antivirus software with cloud capabilities can access a centralized database in the cloud, providing instant access to the latest threat information and signatures. This ensures that the antivirus software is equipped with the most up-to-date knowledge to detect and neutralize emerging threats. Think of it as a network of digital informants constantly sharing intelligence to enhance overall security.

The Antivirus Experience: User-Friendly Protection

In the realm of user experience, antivirus software aims to be a silent guardian, seamlessly operating in the background without disrupting the user's digital activities. Here's how antivirus software enhances the user experience:

Real-Time Protection

Modern antivirus solutions often feature real-time protection, constantly monitoring files, downloads, and web activities in the background. Users may not even be aware of the software's presence, but it acts as an invisible shield, intervening instantly if it detects any potential threats. This unobtrusive vigilance allows users to navigate the digital landscape with confidence.

User-Friendly Interfaces

Antivirus software developers recognize the importance of simplicity in user interfaces. Most antivirus solutions feature intuitive dashboards that provide clear information about the security status of the device. Users can easily initiate scans, review threat reports, and customize settings without delving into complex technical details. The goal is to empower users to manage their digital security effortlessly.

Automated Updates

Keeping antivirus software up-to-date is critical for effective protection. To streamline this process, many antivirus solutions offer automated updates. This ensures that the software receives the latest threat signatures, heuristic algorithms, and other security enhancements without requiring user intervention. Automatic updates contribute to the seamless and continuous strengthening of the digital defense.

Low Resource Impact

Antivirus software strives to provide robust protection without unduly impacting system performance. Developers optimize their software to operate efficiently in the background, minimizing resource usage while still delivering effective security. This balance ensures that users can enjoy a responsive and smooth digital experience without compromising on protection.

The Constant Evolution: Adapting to Emerging Threats

In this environment, the adaptability of antivirus software is crucial. Cybercriminals continually refine their tactics, introducing new and sophisticated threats. Antivirus software developers respond by evolving their strategies and incorporating advanced technologies to counter emerging challenges. Here are key aspects of this ongoing evolution:

Machine Learning and Artificial Intelligence

Machine learning and artificial intelligence (AI) have become integral components of advanced antivirus solutions. These technologies enable the software to learn from patterns and behaviors, improving its ability to identify and respond to new and evolving threats. Machine learning algorithms can analyze vast datasets to detect anomalies and predict potential threats, enhancing the software's intelligence over time.

Threat Intelligence Sharing

Antivirus software is not limited to individual devices; it can also contribute to collective cybersecurity efforts. Threat intelligence sharing involves the exchange of information about emerging threats and vulnerabilities among different security solutions. By participating in these collaborative networks, antivirus software can contribute to a broader defense ecosystem, ensuring that the collective knowledge of the cybersecurity community stays ahead of malicious actors.

Advanced Endpoint Protection

Traditional antivirus software focused primarily on detecting and removing malicious software from devices. However, the concept of endpoint protection has evolved to encompass a broader range of threats. Advanced endpoint protection solutions may include features such as firewall management, device control, and vulnerability assessment, providing a holistic defense strategy that goes beyond traditional boundaries.

Zero-Day Threat Mitigation

Zero-day threats, which exploit vulnerabilities that are unknown to software vendors or security providers, pose a significant challenge. Antivirus software addresses this by employing advanced threat detection techniques, heuristic analysis, and behavioral monitoring to identify and neutralize previously unknown threats. The goal is to mitigate the risk posed by vulnerabilities before they can be exploited.

Challenges and Future Frontiers: Navigating the Cybersecurity Landscape

While antivirus software has proven to be a formidable defender against a wide range of digital threats, challenges persist in the ever-evolving cybersecurity landscape. New attack vectors, sophisticated techniques, and the increasing scale of cyber threats necessitate continuous innovation. Here are some challenges and future frontiers in the realm of antivirus software:

File less Malware and Advanced Evasion Techniques

File less malware, which operates in memory without leaving traces on disk, poses a challenge to traditional antivirus approaches that rely on file-based detection. Antivirus software must evolve to detect and mitigate these stealthy adversaries using techniques such as behavior analysis and memory scanning.

Internet of Things (IoT) Security

As the IoT ecosystem grows, securing connected devices becomes a critical frontier. Antivirus solutions need to extend their protection beyond traditional computing devices to safeguard smart homes, wearables, and industrial IoT systems. This expansion requires considerations for diverse device architectures and communication protocols.

Ransomware Resilience

Ransomware attacks continue to evolve, targeting individuals, businesses, and critical infrastructure. Antivirus software must enhance its resilience against Ransomware by integrating features such as behavior monitoring, anomaly detection, and secure backup solutions to mitigate the impact of attacks.

User Education and Cyber Hygiene

User awareness and cyber hygiene play a pivotal role in the effectiveness of antivirus software. Educating users about safe online practices, recognizing phishing attempts, and understanding the importance of regular updates contributes to building a robust human firewall that complements the digital defenses provided by antivirus solutions.

Chapter 3

PASSWORD MANAGEMENT

BEST PRACTICES FOR PASSWORD CREATION

In the vast digital landscape where our virtual identities are secured by strings of characters, the art and science of password creation play a pivotal role in safeguarding our personal and professional information. Crafting robust and memorable passwords is akin to fortifying the digital moats that protect our sensitive information from the prying eyes of cyber adversaries. Let's delve into the best practices for password creation, unraveling the nuances of constructing shields that balance security and usability.

Complexity is Key

The first pillar of effective password creation lies in embracing complexity. A robust password should be a tapestry of unpredictability, weaving together a mix of uppercase and lowercase letters, numbers, and special characters. This complexity adds a layer of resilience against brute-force attacks, where automated tools attempt to crack passwords by systematically trying every possible combination. Consider creating a passphrase that incorporates a combination of words, numbers, and symbols, ensuring a blend of unpredictability that stands as a formidable defense.

The Longevity of Security

While complexity is crucial, the length of a password is equally significant. Longer passwords inherently provide a broader canvas for complexity, making them more resistant to brute-force and dictionary attacks. Aim for a minimum of 12 characters, and consider pushing the boundaries further for critical accounts. Length acts as a force multiplier, amplifying the strength of your password in the face of evolving cyber threats.

Unique for Every Citadel

In the realm of password management, the cardinal rule is to avoid recycling passwords across multiple platforms. Each digital citadel, whether it's your email, social media, or online banking, deserves a unique key. Reusing passwords across different accounts poses a substantial risk; if one account is compromised, the security of others becomes vulnerable. Embrace the diversity of uniqueness, crafting distinct passwords tailored for each digital fortress you inhabit.

Avoiding the Familiar

Resist the temptation to use easily guessable information in your passwords. Avoid incorporating common words, phrases, or personal details such as birthdays, names, or addresses. Cyber adversaries often employ sophisticated algorithms that can swiftly unravel passwords based on known patterns. By steering clear of the familiar, you erect barriers that thwart these attempts, enhancing the overall resilience of your passwords.

Passphrases

Passphrases represent a user-friendly evolution in password creation. Instead of a string of seemingly random characters, passphrases involve a combination of words or a sentence. This approach not only enhances memorability but also contributes to increased length and complexity. Construct a passphrase that holds personal significance while remaining obscure to others. Consider incorporating a mix of uppercase letters, numbers, and symbols within the passphrase to elevate its security posture.

Regular Reinforcements

Even the most impregnable fortresses require periodic reinforcement. Regularly updating your passwords serves as a proactive defense strategy. Set a routine for changing passwords, especially for high-security accounts. This practice ensures that even if a password is compromised, the window of vulnerability is minimized. Embrace a mindset of continuous improvement, fortifying your digital defenses through regular password updates.

Two-Factor Authentication (2FA)

Two-factor authentication stands as a formidable ally in the realm of password security. This additional layer of defense requires users to provide a second form of verification, often in the form of a code sent to a mobile device or generated by an authenticator app. embrace 2FA wherever possible, as it acts as a vigilant guardian at the gate, demanding dual authentication before granting access. This dynamic duo of passwords and additional verification enhances the overall security posture of your accounts.

Password Managers

Navigating the labyrinth of unique, complex passwords for each digital domain can be a daunting task. This is where password managers emerge as indispensable custodians. Password management tools not only store your passwords securely but also generate and auto fill complex passwords for you. They eliminate the need to remember an extensive array of passwords, empowering users to focus on crafting masterful passphrases for their password manager, which becomes the singular key to unlock the myriad digital gates.

Mindful Sharing

In the interconnected landscape of digital interactions, occasions may arise when sharing passwords becomes necessary. Exercise utmost caution in such situations. If sharing is unavoidable, do so through secure channels, and consider using temporary passwords with limited validity. Always communicate passwords directly and avoid storing them in easily accessible formats. The wisdom of caution in password sharing minimizes the risk of unauthorized access.

Security Hygiene

Password creation is just one facet of a broader security hygiene regimen. Regularly review and update your security settings, be wary of phishing attempts, and stay informed about emerging cybersecurity threats. A holistic approach to security involves being vigilant across all facets of your digital presence, creating a layered defense that goes beyond the strength of passwords alone.

PASSWORD STORAGE AND PROTECTION

In the intricate tapestry of digital security, where our virtual identities are safeguarded by strings of characters, the question of password storage and protection takes center stage. As the guardians of our digital fortresses, passwords demand a secure abode, shielded from the prying eyes of cyber adversaries. Let's embark on a journey to unravel the nuances of password storage and protection, exploring the methodologies and practices that fortify this critical aspect of our online defense.

The Encryption Paradox: Transforming Security

At the heart of secure password storage lies the paradox of encryption—an artful dance of transforming sensitive information into an unintelligible cipher. Encryption ensures that even if unauthorized entities gain access to stored passwords, the information appears as a scrambled and unreadable sequence of characters. Two primary encryption methods dominate the realm of password security:

- Hashing: This one-way transformation involves converting a password into a fixed-length string of characters. The irreversible nature of hashing ensures that even if the hashed value is compromised, it is computationally infeasible to reverse the process and reveal the original password. Common hashing algorithms include SHA-256 and crypt.

- Salting: To enhance the security of hashed passwords, a unique random value known as a "salt" is added before hashing. Salting prevents the use of recomputed tables (rainbow tables) for password cracking, adding an extra layer of defense against attacks.

Hashed and Salted

The marriage of hashing and salting forms a dynamic duo that fortifies password storage. When a user creates or updates a password, the system generates a unique salt, combines it with the password, and then applies the hashing algorithm. The resulting hashed and salted password, along with the salt, is stored in the database. During the authentication process, the system retrieves the salt, combines it with the entered password, and hashes the result for comparison with the stored value. This approach mitigates the risks associated with hashed passwords and elevates the overall security posture.

Storage on the Server

The server serves as the citadel where encrypted passwords are stored, standing guard against potential breaches. Implementing robust security measures on the server is paramount. Access controls, encryption protocols, and regular security audits contribute to fortifying this digital bastion. The server's responsibility extends beyond storage— it must validate authentication requests, ensuring that the entered password, when hashed and salted, matches the stored value.

Secure Communication Channels

As passwords traverse the digital bridges between user devices and servers, the channels of communication must be fortified to prevent interception by malicious actors. Implementing secure communication protocols, such as HTTPS, encrypts data in transit, shielding it from eavesdroppers. This ensures that passwords remain confidential during the authentication process, adding an essential layer of protection.

Password Policies

Password storage is intrinsically linked to the creation and management of passwords. Establishing and enforcing robust password policies contributes to the overall security ecosystem. Policies may include requirements for password complexity, minimum length, and expiration intervals. By nurturing security hygiene through well-crafted policies, organizations instill a culture of resilience against common password vulnerabilities.

Multi-Factor Authentication (MFA)

While password storage forms the foundational layer of security, fortifying the citadel demands additional sentries. Multi-factor authentication (MFA) stands as a stalwart ally in this endeavor. MFA requires users to provide a secondary form of verification—such as a code sent to a mobile device or generated by an authenticator app—in addition to their password. This additional layer adds an extra dimension to authentication, reducing the reliance on passwords alone.

User Education

In the symbiotic relationship between users and systems, education emerges as a powerful catalyst for security. Users, as the defenders of their digital identities, must be empowered with knowledge about secure password practices. Educating users on the importance of strong, unique passwords, the risks of password reuse, and the significance of timely updates contributes to a resilient human firewall.

Encryption Key Management

In the realm of encryption, the security of passwords hinges on the management of encryption keys. Encryption keys are essential components that unlock the cryptographic vaults where passwords reside. Implementing robust key management practices, including secure storage and regular rotation of keys, ensures that the sentry's key ring remains impenetrable.

Regular Audits and Monitoring

Vigilance is the cornerstone of effective password storage. Regular security audits and monitoring mechanisms act as watchful guardians, scanning for signs of unauthorized access or anomalous activities. These audits encompass not only the storage and retrieval of passwords but also the broader landscape of authentication and user account management.

MULTI-FACTOR AUTHENTICATION

In the sprawling landscape of digital security, where the guardianship of our virtual identities is paramount, multi- factor authentication (MFA) emerges as a stalwart defender. MFA is the embodiment of a robust defense strategy, a multifaceted shield that stands between our sensitive information and the ever-present threats of cyber adversaries.

Let's embark on a journey through the intricate realms of MFA, unraveling its essence, exploring its mechanisms, and understanding its significance in the dynamic landscape of cybersecurity.

The Essence of Multi-Factor Authentication

At its core, multi-factor authentication transcends the limitations of traditional password-based security. In a world where passwords, despite their complexities, can be vulnerable to various cyber threats, MFA introduces additional layers of verification. It's a recognition that relying solely on something known (like a password) has its limitations. MFA introduces a dynamic dance of factors— something you know, something you have, and something you are—creating a robust triad that fortifies the authentication process.

The Factors Unveiled

Understanding the factors that constitute multi-factor authentication is pivotal in grasping its effectiveness. These include:

Knowledge Factor (Something You Know)

This is the traditional realm of passwords and PINs. Users authenticate themselves by providing something they know— typically a combination of characters that serve as a secret key. While knowledge factors remain a fundamental part of authentication, MFA enriches this by combining it with other factors.

Possession Factor (Something You Have)

The possession factor introduces a tangible element into the authentication equation. It involves having a physical device or token that serves as a second layer of verification. This could be a smartphone, a hardware token, or a smart card. Authenticating with something you have adds a layer of security, as even if someone obtains your password, they would still need the physical token to access your account.

Inherence Factor (Something You Are)

Inherence factors involve biometric markers unique to an individual—fingerprints, facial recognition, voice patterns, or even retina scans. These biological or behavioral attributes serve as a highly personalized and distinctive element of authentication. Inherence factors add a layer of sophistication, making it exceedingly challenging for unauthorized entities to mimic or replicate.

The Dance of Authentication: How MFA Works

The orchestration of multi-factor authentication involves a choreographed dance between these factors, creating a dynamic and resilient authentication process:

Step 1: Something You Know (Knowledge Factor)

The user initiates the authentication process by entering a password or PIN, providing the foundational layer of verification.

Step 2: Something You Have (Possession Factor)

Following the password entry, the user is prompted to provide a second form of verification. This could be a code generated by a mobile app, a text message sent to a registered phone, or the insertion of a physical security token.

Step 3: Something You Are (Inherence Factor)

The final layer involves an inherent element, typically a biometric scan. This could be a fingerprint scan, facial recognition, or another biometric identifier. The system validates the biometric data against the stored profile, completing the multi-factor authentication process.

This dance of authentication, incorporating diverse factors, elevates the security posture beyond the confines of traditional single-factor methods. It introduces complexity and diversity, making unauthorized access significantly more challenging.

The Significance of MFA: Strengthening the Digital Moat

Multi-factor authentication is more than a security feature; it's a fundamental paradigm shift in how we approach digital authentication. Its significance resonates across various dimensions of cybersecurity:

Mitigating Password Vulnerabilities

One of the primary vulnerabilities in traditional authentication methods lies in the reliance on passwords. Passwords, even when complex, can be susceptible to brute- force attacks, phishing, and other tactics. MFA mitigates these vulnerabilities by requiring additional factors beyond the password.

Enhancing User Verification

MFA enhances the confidence in user verification. By combining multiple factors, it significantly reduces the risk of unauthorized access. Even if one factor is compromised, the additional layers act as a formidable defense.

Adapting to Evolving Threats

The threat landscape in cybersecurity is dynamic, with adversaries continually refining their tactics. MFA provides a flexible defense mechanism that adapts to emerging threats. As new vulnerabilities are identified, MFA can evolve to address them, making it a resilient strategy in the face of evolving cyber threats.

Protecting Sensitive Transactions

In scenarios where sensitive transactions or access to critical systems are involved, MFA becomes a non-negotiable layer of protection. It ensures that only authorized individuals, with possession of the requisite physical or biometric elements, can initiate such actions.

Compliance Requirements

Many regulatory frameworks and industry standards mandate the use of multi-factor authentication, especially in sectors dealing with sensitive information such as finance, healthcare, and government. Adhering to these compliance requirements not only strengthens security but also ensures alignment with legal and regulatory frameworks.

MFA in Action: Real-World Scenarios

The real-world application of multi-factor authentication extends across a spectrum of scenarios, each showcasing its efficacy:

Online Accounts

Many online platforms, including email services, social media, and financial institutions, offer MFA options. Users can enable MFA for their accounts, adding an extra layer of protection beyond passwords.

Enterprise Security

In corporate environments, MFA is a cornerstone of robust cybersecurity policies. Employees may be required to authenticate using a combination of passwords, security tokens, and biometric scans to access sensitive systems or data.

Remote Access

With the prevalence of remote work, securing remote access to corporate networks has become paramount. MFA serves as a critical defense, ensuring that only authorized personnel with the necessary credentials and verification methods can access corporate resources remotely.

Financial Transactions

Online banking and financial transactions often incorporate MFA to safeguard against unauthorized access and fraudulent activities. This is particularly crucial given the sensitive nature of financial information.

Healthcare Systems

In the healthcare sector, where patient data is highly sensitive, MFA is employed to secure access to electronic health records (EHRs) and other critical systems. This ensures that only authorized healthcare professionals can access patient information.

Challenges and Considerations: Balancing Security and Usability

While MFA is a powerful tool in the cybersecurity arsenal, it is not without its challenges. Balancing security with usability is a delicate dance, and organizations must navigate certain considerations:

User Experience

Striking a balance between security and a seamless user experience is critical. Cumbersome or overly complex MFA processes may lead to user frustration and resistance. Designing user-friendly MFA experiences is essential to encourage widespread adoption.

Implementation Complexity

Deploying MFA across an organization requires careful planning and implementation. Integration with existing systems, user training, and ensuring compatibility with various devices and platforms can pose challenges.

Biometric Privacy Concerns

The use of biometric data raises privacy concerns. Organizations implementing biometric authentication must adhere to stringent privacy standards, ensuring the secure storage and responsible handling of biometric information.

Device Dependency

Some MFA methods, particularly those involving possession factors, are dependent on the availability and security of user devices. Organizations must consider scenarios where users may not have access to their primary devices.

Phishing and Social Engineering

While MFA mitigates many forms of cyber threats, it is not entirely immune to phishing or social engineering attacks. Adversaries may attempt to trick users into providing MFA codes or bypassing authentication through manipulative tactics.

Future Frontiers: Advancements in MFA Technology

As technology advances, the landscape of multi-factor authentication continues to evolve. Emerging trends and technologies are shaping the future frontiers of MFA:

Biometric Advancements

Ongoing advancements in biometric technology, such as behavioral biometrics and continuous authentication, enhance the accuracy and security of biometric authentication methods.

Zero Trust Architecture

The concept of Zero Trust, where trust is never assumed and verification is required from anyone trying to access resources, aligns closely with MFA principles. Zero Trust Architecture is gaining prominence as a holistic security framework.

Contextual Authentication

Context-aware authentication considers additional factors such as the user's location, device posture, and behavior patterns to assess the risk level. This adaptive approach enhances security by adjusting authentication requirements based on the context.

Password less Authentication

The move towards password less authentication aims to eliminate reliance on traditional passwords altogether. Instead, it leverages factors such as biometrics, possession of a trusted device, or cryptographic keys for seamless and secure authentication.

Blockchain-Based Authentication

Some solutions explore the use of blockchain technology to enhance the security and transparency of authentication processes. Blockchain can provide a decentralized and tamper-resistant ledger for authentication events.

Chapter 4

PRIVACY AND SECURITY

UNDERSTANDING THE IMPORTANCE OF PRIVACY

The importance of privacy emerges as a cornerstone of individual rights and societal well-being. Privacy is not merely a luxury or a preference; it is a fundamental human right that underpins the dignity, autonomy, and freedom of individuals. As we navigate the digital highways and byways, understanding and championing the significance of privacy becomes imperative, shaping not only our personal interactions but also the broader fabric of society.

The Essence of Privacy: Beyond Secrecy

Privacy is often misconstrued as synonymous with secrecy—a realm reserved for concealing personal information or actions. While secrecy is an aspect of privacy, the concept is far more nuanced and expansive. At its essence, privacy encompasses the right to control one's personal information, decisions, and boundaries. It is a dynamic and multifaceted concept that extends across various dimensions of our lives, both online and offline.

Autonomy and Individual Agency

At the heart of privacy lies the notion of autonomy— the ability of individuals to govern their own lives, make choices free from unwarranted interference, and define the boundaries of their personal space. Privacy empowers individuals with agency, allowing them to navigate the complexities of their existence with a sense of control and self- determination. When privacy is respected, individuals can shape their identities, form relationships, and pursue their aspirations without the looming threat of external intrusion.

Personal Space in the Digital Age: Navigating the Virtual Realms

In the digital age, where our interactions, communications, and even our thoughts leave digital footprints, the concept of personal space has transcended physical boundaries. Online platforms, social media, and digital services have become extensions of our lives, blurring the lines between the physical and virtual realms. The importance of privacy in this context lies in safeguarding the integrity of our digital personas, preserving the right to explore, express, and connect without undue surveillance or manipulation.

Dignity and the Right to Be Forgotten: Redefining Narratives

Privacy is intricately linked to human dignity—the intrinsic value and worth of each individual. The right to be forgotten, a pivotal aspect of privacy, allows individuals to reshape their narratives and move forward without the perpetual shadow of past actions or circumstances. This right acknowledges that individuals evolve, learn, and grow, and they should not be perpetually defined by their historical digital imprints.

Trust in Relationships: The Foundation of Societal Bonds

Privacy forms the bedrock of trust in interpersonal relationships, whether they be familial, romantic, or friendships. The ability to confide, share, and communicate openly relies on the assurance that personal disclosures will be respected and protected. In a society where trust is nurtured through respectful privacy practices, individuals feel secure in forming meaningful connections and expressing their authentic selves.

Privacy as a Check on Power: Balancing Asymmetries

Privacy acts as a crucial check on power imbalances within societal structures. In contexts where there is a concentration of authority, whether in governmental institutions, corporations, or other entities, the erosion of privacy can lead to unchecked surveillance and control. Upholding privacy rights ensures a balance of power, preventing overreach and fostering a society where individuals are not subject to unwarranted scrutiny or manipulation.

Psychological Well-being: Unplugging from the Surveillance Society

The constant gaze of surveillance, both overt and covert, can have profound implications for psychological well-being. The awareness of being under constant scrutiny, whether by entities or individuals, can contribute to stress, anxiety, and a sense of vulnerability. Preserving privacy provides a reprieve, allowing individuals to exist without the weight of constant observation, fostering mental and emotional resilience.

Privacy in the Face of Technological Advances: Adapting to the Digital Landscape

As technology advances at an unprecedented pace, the importance of privacy takes center stage. The digital landscape, with its myriad conveniences and innovations, also introduces new challenges to privacy. Surveillance technologies, data collection practices, and the increasing interconnectivity of devices raise concerns about the erosion of personal space. Understanding the implications of these technological shifts is crucial in navigating a future where privacy remains a fundamental right.

Data Protection and Privacy Laws: Safeguarding Rights

In response to the evolving digital landscape, governments and international bodies have recognized the need for robust data protection and privacy laws. Legislation such as the General Data Protection Regulation (GDPR) in Europe seek to establish frameworks that empower individuals with control over their personal data. These laws reinforce the idea that privacy is not just a personal preference but a legal right deserving of protection.

Privacy Challenges in the Social Media Era: Striking a Balance

The rise of social media has reshaped the dynamics of privacy, introducing both opportunities for connection and challenges to personal boundaries. Individuals willingly share aspects of their lives on these platforms, contributing to a digital tapestry of collective experiences. However, the commodification of personal data, the potential for information misuse, and the blurring of public and private spheres underscore the need for mindful navigation and informed choices in the social media era.

Surveillance Capitalism: The Intersection of Profit and Privacy

In the digital economy, a concept known as surveillance capitalism has emerged, where user data becomes a commodity for profit. The services we use, often offered for free, are sustained by the collection and analysis of our personal information. Navigating this landscape requires an awareness of the trade-offs between convenience and privacy, prompting individuals to question the extent to which their data is being commoditized.

Ethical Considerations in Data Use: Respecting Individual Narratives

Ethical considerations in data use extend beyond legal compliance. Organizations and entities handling personal data bear a responsibility to ensure ethical data practices. This involves transparent communication with users, obtaining informed consent, and respecting the ethical boundaries that uphold individual narratives and rights.

Education and Digital Literacy: Empowering Privacy Advocates

As privacy becomes a central theme in the digital discourse, promoting education and digital literacy is paramount. Empowering individuals to understand the implications of their digital footprint, make informed choices about privacy settings, and advocate for their rights contributes to a collective ethos of privacy consciousness.

The Intersection of Privacy and Security: A Symbiotic Relationship

Privacy and security share an intricate relationship, each reinforcing the other. While privacy safeguards personal information from unauthorized access, security measures ensure the integrity and confidentiality of that information. The symbiotic nature of this relationship highlights the interconnectedness of individual rights and broader societal well-being.

Privacy by Design: Integrating Privacy into Technological Development

The concept of privacy by design advocates for the integration of privacy considerations at the inception of technological development. By embedding privacy principles into the design and architecture of digital systems, developers and innovators can create products and services that prioritize user rights and data protection.

PRIVACY AND SECURITY CONSIDERATIONS

In the intricate dance between technology and our daily lives, the considerations of privacy and security emerge as crucial factors that shape the contours of our digital experiences. These considerations go beyond mere buzzwords; they represent fundamental principles that underpin our interactions in an interconnected world. As we navigate the realms of social media, online transactions, and smart devices, understanding the delicate balance between privacy and security becomes paramount. This exploration delves into the human-centric aspects of these considerations, steering away from technical jargon to illuminate the broader implications for individuals, organizations, and society as a whole.

The Tapestry of Privacy

Privacy, in its essence, is about personal boundaries— the right to control one's personal information and the autonomy to decide what aspects of one's life are shared with others. In the digital age, where our every click, like, and purchase leaves a digital footprint, the tapestry of privacy extends beyond physical spaces into the vast expanse of the online world. It is a realm where individuals navigate the delicate balance between sharing and safeguarding, seeking to express themselves while preserving a sense of autonomy.

Security as a Sentinel: Safeguarding the Digital Citadel

Security, on the other hand, is the sentinel that stands guard over the digital citadel. It encompasses the measures and protocols in place to protect information, systems, and networks from unauthorized access, breaches, or malicious activities. While privacy is about personal boundaries, security is the mechanism that ensures these boundaries are respected and fortified. It is the guardian that shields individuals and organizations from the myriad threats that lurk in the digital landscape.

The Interplay of Privacy and Security

Privacy and security are not isolated concepts but are intricately interwoven in a symbiotic dance. Imagine privacy as the individual's desire to keep a journal secure, and security as the lock and key that protect the journal from prying eyes. The absence of either compromises the integrity of the system. In the digital realm, the interplay of privacy and security becomes even more critical as individuals share vast amounts of personal information online.

The Human Element: Trust as the Cornerstone

At the core of the interplay between privacy and security lies the human element—trust. Individuals share their personal information online, conduct financial transactions, and engage in social interactions based on a foundation of trust. Trust in the digital realm is contingent on the assurance that privacy will be respected and that security measures are in place to safeguard against breaches. Organizations, platforms, and service providers play a pivotal role in fostering and maintaining this trust.

Navigating the Digital Landscape: Challenges and Considerations

As we navigate the digital landscape, certain challenges and considerations come to the forefront, demanding our attention and strategic responses:

Data Breaches and Vulnerabilities

High-profile data breaches have become all too familiar, underscoring the vulnerability of digital systems. From financial institutions to social media platforms, the specter of data breaches highlights the critical need for robust security measures to protect against unauthorized access.

User Consent and Control

With the proliferation of data-driven services, the issue of user consent and control over personal information becomes paramount. Individuals must be empowered to make informed choices about what data they share and retain control over how that data is used.

Surveillance and Privacy Erosion

The omnipresence of surveillance technologies, both by governments and private entities, raises concerns about erosion of privacy. Striking a balance between legitimate security concerns and preserving individual privacy rights is a delicate endeavor that requires thoughtful consideration.

Ethical Use of Data

The ethical considerations surrounding the use of personal data loom large in the digital age. Organizations must grapple with questions of transparency, accountability, and the responsible handling of user information to ensure that ethical standards are upheld.

User Education and Awareness

Nurturing a culture of privacy and security begins with user education and awareness. Individuals need to understand the implications of their online activities, the importance of strong passwords, and the potential risks associated with sharing sensitive information.

Privacy by Design: Infusing Ethics into Technological Architecture

The concept of privacy by design advocates for the integration of privacy considerations at the forefront of technological development. It is a proactive approach that seeks to embed privacy principles into the architecture and design of digital systems. By incorporating privacy from the inception of a product or service, developers can mitigate potential privacy risks and foster a culture of ethical data handling.

The Human-Centric Approach: Beyond Compliance

While regulations such as the General Data Protection Regulation (GDPR) set legal frameworks for data protection, a truly human-centric approach goes beyond mere compliance. It involves a commitment to ethical practices, transparent communication, and a genuine respect for user rights. Organizations that prioritize these principles not only comply with regulations but also build trust with their user base.

Personal Responsibility in the Digital Age: Empowering Users

Empowering individuals with a sense of personal responsibility in the digital age is central to cultivating a privacy-conscious culture. Users play a pivotal role in safeguarding their own privacy by adopting secure practices, being vigilant about online activities, and making informed choices about the platforms and services they engage with. Education and awareness campaigns can serve as catalysts for empowering users to become active participants in their own digital well-being.

Emerging Technologies: Ethical Considerations in Innovation

As emerging technologies such as artificial intelligence, machine learning, and the Internet of Things continue to reshape the digital landscape, ethical considerations become paramount. The potential for intrusive data collection, algorithmic bias, and unintended consequences underscores the need for ethical frameworks that guide the development and deployment of these technologies. Innovators must navigate the ethical dimensions of technological advancement to ensure that progress aligns with human values and rights.

Striking a Balance: Privacy, Security, and Innovation

Striking a balance between privacy, security, and innovation requires a nuanced approach. While robust security measures are essential for safeguarding information, overly restrictive privacy measures may stifle innovation.

Finding the equilibrium involves fostering a culture where privacy and security are seen not as impediments but as enablers of innovation. This balance is particularly critical in sectors such as healthcare, finance, and research, where technological advancements can yield transformative benefits.

The Intersection of Privacy and Digital Commerce: Building Trust

In the realm of digital commerce, where transactions and interactions unfold across online platforms, the intersection of privacy and security is a cornerstone of building trust. E-commerce relies on individuals feeling secure in sharing their payment information, personal details, and preferences. Ensuring robust security measures and transparent privacy practices is not just a regulatory requirement but a business imperative that fosters customer trust and loyalty.

Privacy and Security in the Workplace: Balancing Oversight and Respect

The workplace is a microcosm where privacy and security considerations intersect with the dynamics of employee oversight and respect. Employers must strike a delicate balance between implementing security measures to protect sensitive corporate information and respecting the privacy rights of employees. Transparent communication about data handling practices, clear policies, and an acknowledgment of employee rights contribute to fostering a workplace environment that values both security and privacy.

Privacy in the Age of Social Media: Navigating the Sharing Landscape

The ubiquitous nature of social media platforms has reshaped the landscape of personal sharing. Individuals willingly share aspects of their lives, opinions, and preferences on these platforms, contributing to a collective digital tapestry. Navigating this landscape involves understanding the privacy settings, being mindful of oversharing, and recognizing the potential consequences of digital footprints. Social media platforms, in turn, bear a responsibility to prioritize user privacy and security.

Resilience in the Face of Cyber Threats: Collective Vigilance

In an era where cyber threats constantly evolve, resilience becomes a collective endeavor. Organizations, governments, and individuals must remain vigilant, adopting proactive security measures, staying informed about emerging threats, and fostering a culture of resilience. This collective vigilance extends beyond technical defenses to include a commitment to ethical practices and a respect for the privacy rights of individuals.

The Road Ahead: Ethical Innovation and Inclusive Conversations

As we traverse the road ahead, the considerations of privacy and security will continue to evolve in tandem with technological advancements. Ethical innovation, inclusive conversations, and a commitment to human-centric principles will shape the way forward. It is a journey that involves not just technological expertise but a profound understanding of the human experience in the digital age.

PRIVACY LAWS AND REGULATIONS

In the intricate tapestry of the digital age, where personal information is exchanged in the blink of an eye and transactions unfold seamlessly across online platforms, the need for robust privacy laws and regulations has become increasingly apparent. These legal frameworks serve as the guardians of individual rights in the vast expanse of the digital landscape, aiming to strike a delicate balance between innovation, convenience, and the protection of sensitive personal data. This exploration delves into the realm of privacy laws and regulations, unraveling the complexities in a human-like narrative that demystifies the legal jargon and highlights the profound implications for individuals, businesses, and society at large.

The Foundation of Privacy Laws: Safeguarding Individual Rights

At the heart of privacy laws lies a fundamental recognition—the acknowledgment that individuals have a right to control their personal information. These laws establish a legal framework that delineates the boundaries within which organizations and entities can collect, process, and share personal data. The foundation of privacy laws is rooted in the principles of autonomy, dignity, and the belief that individuals should have a say in how their information is used in the digital realm.

Global Perspectives: A Mosaic of Privacy Regulations

Privacy laws and regulations are not uniform across the globe; rather, they form a mosaic of diverse approaches influenced by cultural, legal, and societal nuances. In Europe, the General Data Protection Regulation (GDPR) stands as a beacon, setting high standards for data protection and privacy. The GDPR empowers individuals with control over their personal data and imposes stringent requirements on organizations handling such data. In the United States, a patchwork of privacy laws exists, with variations between federal and state regulations. States like California have taken a pioneering step with the California Consumer Privacy Act (CCPA), providing residents with rights over their personal information.

The Genesis of Privacy Laws: Responding to Technological Evolution

The genesis of privacy laws can be traced to the accelerated pace of technological evolution. As the digital landscape expanded, so did the concerns about the misuse and exploitation of personal data. From the early days of the internet to the era of social media and sophisticated data analytics, lawmakers recognized the need for legal frameworks that could adapt to the dynamic nature of technology. Privacy laws, therefore, emerged as a response to the evolving challenges of the digital age, aiming to provide individuals with a shield against potential abuses of their personal information.

The Pillars of Privacy Laws: Key Principles Unveiled

Privacy laws are anchored in a set of key principles that serve as guiding lights in the protection of personal data:

Consent and Transparency

One of the cornerstones of privacy laws is the principle of informed consent. Individuals must be informed about how their data will be used, and they should have the opportunity to consent or opt-out. Transparency is paramount, ensuring that organizations are open about their data practices.

Purpose Limitation

Personal data should be collected for specified, explicit, and legitimate purposes. Privacy laws emphasize the importance of organizations defining clear purposes for data collection and ensuring that data is not used in ways that are incompatible with those purposes.

Data Minimization

The concept of data minimization underscores the idea that organizations should only collect the data that is strictly necessary for the purposes for which it is processed. This principle aims to prevent the unnecessary collection of excessive or irrelevant information.

Accuracy

Privacy laws emphasize the accuracy of personal data. Organizations are expected to take reasonable steps to ensure that the information they hold is accurate and up-to-date. Individuals should have the right to rectify inaccuracies in their personal data.

Storage Limitation

Personal data should not be kept for longer than necessary for the purposes for which it was collected. Privacy laws prescribe limits on the retention of data, promoting responsible data management practices.

Security and Integrity

Organizations are obligated to implement appropriate security measures to protect personal data from unauthorized access, disclosure, alteration, and destruction. Maintaining the integrity and confidentiality of personal information is a foundational aspect of privacy laws.

GDPR: A Landmark in Data Protection

The General Data Protection Regulation (GDPR), enacted by the European Union, stands as a landmark in the realm of data protection. Enforced in May 2018, the GDPR represents a paradigm shift in how personal data is handled. Its key provisions empower individuals with unprecedented control over their data. The right to be informed, the right to access, the right to rectification, and the right to erasure are among the rights bestowed upon individuals under the GDPR. Organizations that process personal data are held accountable, facing substantial fines for non-compliance.

CCPA: Pioneering Privacy Rights in the United States

In the United States, the California Consumer Privacy Act (CCPA) has emerged as a trailblazer in privacy legislation. Enacted in 2018 and becoming operative in 2020, the CCPA grants California residents significant rights over their personal information. The right to know what personal information is collected, the right to delete that information, and the right to opt-out of the sale of personal data are central tenets of the CCPA. The law applies not only to businesses physically located in California but also to those that conduct business with California residents on a significant scale.

Sector-Specific Regulations: Tailoring Privacy Rules

In addition to overarching privacy laws, various sectors have implemented specific regulations tailored to their unique characteristics. In healthcare, the Health Insurance Portability and Accountability Act (HIPAA) regulates the use and disclosure of protected health information. In the financial sector, the Gramm-Leach-Bliley Act (GLBA) addresses the privacy of consumer financial information. These sector-specific regulations recognize that different industries handle distinct types of sensitive information, requiring specialized safeguards.

Evolving Landscape: Amendments and Iterations

The privacy landscape is not static; it evolves in response to emerging challenges and technological advancements. Privacy laws are subject to amendments and iterations to address gaps, enhance protections, and adapt to the changing needs of society. For example, the California Privacy Rights Act (CPRA) builds upon the CCPA, introducing additional privacy rights and establishing a dedicated agency for enforcement. These iterative changes reflect a commitment to staying ahead of the curve in the ever- shifting terrain of digital privacy.

Global Collaboration: Navigating Cross- Border Data Flows

In a world where data knows no borders, the importance of global collaboration in privacy enforcement cannot be overstated. Cross-border data flows necessitate harmonized approaches to privacy to ensure consistent protections for individuals. Initiatives such as the APEC Privacy Framework and the Privacy Shield (now invalidated) aimed to facilitate the secure flow of personal data between regions. The global dialogue on privacy fosters cooperation and shared principles in the face of transnational data challenges.

Enforcement Mechanisms: Holding Entities Accountable

Privacy laws are only as effective as their enforcement mechanisms. Regulatory bodies play a crucial role in holding entities accountable for compliance. In the European Union, Data Protection Authorities (DPAs) are responsible for enforcing the GDPR. In the United States, the Federal Trade Commission (FTC) has taken a central role in privacy enforcement, penalizing organizations for deceptive or unfair practices related to consumer privacy.

Challenges in Enforcement: Navigating the Complex Terrain

While privacy laws establish clear principles and rights, the enforcement landscape is not without challenges. The global nature of data flows can create jurisdictional complexities. The sheer volume of data processed by large tech companies poses challenges in monitoring and regulating their practices. Additionally, the rapid pace of technological innovation often outpaces the ability of regulators to adapt, requiring a dynamic and proactive approach to enforcement.

The Role of Technology: Privacy Enhancing Technologies (PETs)

As technology both challenges and complements privacy laws, Privacy Enhancing Technologies (PETs) emerge as tools to fortify individual privacy. Encryption, anonymization, and differential privacy are examples of PETs that aim to protect personal data while still allowing for meaningful data analysis. The ongoing dialogue between technologists and policymakers seeks to strike a balance, leveraging technology to enhance privacy rather than erode it.

Corporate Responsibility: Ethical Data Practices

Beyond legal compliance, corporate responsibility in the realm of privacy extends to ethical data practices. Organizations that prioritize privacy as a core value go beyond meeting legal requirements—they embrace a commitment to respecting user rights, transparently communicating data practices, and fostering a culture of privacy consciousness. Ethical considerations guide decisions about data collection, use, and sharing, acknowledging the human impact of corporate actions.

Privacy in the Public Sphere: Government Surveillance and Civil Liberties

Privacy laws also intersect with broader debates about government surveillance and civil liberties. Striking a balance between national security imperatives and individual privacy rights remains a complex challenge. The tension between the need for surveillance in the interest of public safety and the protection of citizens' rights underscores the ongoing dialogue about the scope and limits of privacy laws in the public sphere.

The Future of Privacy Laws: Adapting to Technological Frontiers

As we peer into the future, the trajectory of privacy laws will undoubtedly be shaped by the unfolding technological frontiers. Emerging technologies such as artificial intelligence, biometrics, and the Internet of Things pose new challenges that demand innovative legal responses. Privacy laws will need to evolve to address the nuanced implications of these technologies, ensuring that individuals retain control over their personal information in an era of unprecedented connectivity.

DATA PROTECTION AND PRIVACY POLICIES

In the vast realm of the digital landscape, where personal information flows seamlessly across networks and platforms, the concepts of data protection and privacy policies stand as guardians of individual rights and information integrity. These policies, often embedded in the terms and conditions of digital services and organizational practices, shape the way in which personal data is handled, processed, and safeguarded. This exploration delves into the human-centric dimensions of data protection and privacy policies, unraveling their significance, key components, and the implications for individuals navigating the interconnected web of the digital age.

The Essence of Data Protection: Safeguarding Digital Lives

At its core, data protection is about safeguarding the digital lives of individuals. It encompasses the measures and practices in place to ensure that personal data, ranging from names and addresses to more sensitive information like financial details and health records, is handled with care, respect, and a commitment to individual rights. Data protection seeks to strike a balance between the benefits of data-driven services and the need to protect individuals from potential misuse or breaches.

Privacy Policies: The Blueprint for Responsible Data Handling

Privacy policies serve as the blueprint that outlines how organizations, websites, and digital services will handle the personal information entrusted to them by users. These policies, often presented in lengthy and complex documents, articulate the rules of engagement between users and the entities that collect and process their data. While the language of these policies can be daunting, the fundamental purpose is to foster transparency, trust, and informed decision-making among users.

Transparency and Informed Consent: Pillars of Privacy Policies

At the heart of privacy policies lie two pivotal concepts—transparency and informed consent. Transparency requires organizations to be open and honest about how they collect, use, and share personal data. Privacy policies are expected to be clear, concise, and accessible, enabling users to understand the data practices of the entity they are engaging with. Informed consent, on the other hand, empowers individuals to make conscious decisions about the use of their data. Users should have the opportunity to agree or disagree with data collection and processing practices, ensuring that their consent is genuine and informed.

Key Components of Privacy Policies: Decoding the Language

While privacy policies may vary in structure and detail, several key components are commonly found:

Data Collection

Privacy policies detail what types of data are collected from users. This can range from basic contact information to more intricate data such as browsing history, device information, or preferences.

Purpose of Data Processing:

Organizations must specify the purposes for which they collect and process data. Whether it's to provide a service, improve user experience, or personalize content, the purposes should be clearly outlined.

Data Sharing

The disclosure of how and with whom user data may be shared is a critical aspect of privacy policies. This includes sharing with third parties, affiliates, or service providers.

Security Measures

Privacy policies often touch upon the security measures in place to protect user data. This includes encryption, access controls, and other safeguards to prevent unauthorized access or breaches.

Retention Period

The duration for which data will be retained is another essential element. Organizations should specify how long they will keep user data and the criteria used to determine retention periods.

User Rights

Privacy policies should inform users of their rights. This includes the right to access their data, rectify inaccuracies, request deletion, and, in some jurisdictions, the right to data portability.

Cookies and Tracking

Information about the use of cookies and tracking technologies is often included. This section explains how cookies are used, their purpose, and how users can manage their preferences.

Policy Updates

Privacy policies are not static documents. Users should be informed about how and when the policy may be updated. Organizations commit to notifying users of significant changes.

Privacy by Design: Integrating Privacy from the Start

The concept of privacy by design is an integral aspect of responsible data handling. It emphasizes the integration of privacy considerations at the inception of product or service development. Rather than treating privacy as an afterthought, organizations are encouraged to embed privacy features into the design and architecture of their offerings. This proactive approach ensures that privacy is not compromised in the pursuit of technological innovation.

Challenges in Privacy Policies: Navigating Complexity

Despite their importance, privacy policies face challenges that can impede their effectiveness:

Complexity and Length

Privacy policies are notorious for their length and complexity. The language used can be legalistic and challenging for the average user to comprehend. This poses a barrier to informed decision-making.

Consent Fatigue

The prevalence of lengthy terms and conditions across digital services can lead to what is known as "consent fatigue." Users may become accustomed to clicking "agree" without fully understanding or evaluating the implications of data sharing.

Vague Language

Some privacy policies use vague or ambiguous language, making it difficult for users to grasp the specifics of data practices. Clear and precise communication is essential for informed consent.

Lack of Standardization

There is often a lack of standardization in the format and content of privacy policies. This variation can make it challenging for users to compare and understand the data practices of different entities.

Accessibility Issues

Ensuring that privacy policies are accessible to all users, including those with disabilities, is a consideration that is sometimes overlooked. Accessibility is crucial for fostering inclusivity in digital interactions.

Legal Frameworks: Navigating the Patchwork of Regulations

The regulatory landscape for data protection is diverse and often characterized by a patchwork of regulations. Different countries and regions have enacted their own laws, leading to variations in the level of protection afforded to individuals. In Europe, the GDPR stands as a comprehensive and stringent framework, while in the United States, a sectoral and state-specific approach prevails. Navigating this patchwork requires organizations to adopt a nuanced understanding of the legal requirements applicable to their operations.

Privacy Policies in Practice: Bridging the Gap

While privacy policies outline the theoretical framework for data protection, their efficacy in practice depends on several factors:

User Education

Educating users about the importance of privacy, the contents of privacy policies, and how to manage their privacy settings is crucial. This empowerment enables users to make informed choices.

Privacy Tools and Controls

Organizations should provide users with accessible tools and controls to manage their privacy preferences. This includes options for opting out of certain data collection practices or adjusting privacy settings.

Regulatory Compliance

Organizations must not only draft comprehensive privacy policies but also ensure compliance with applicable regulations. This involves staying abreast of legal developments and adjusting policies accordingly.

Accountability and Transparency

Demonstrating accountability and transparency is key. Organizations should be ready to explain their data practices, respond to user queries, and be transparent about any incidents or breaches.

Ethical Data Practices

Beyond legal compliance, organizations should embrace ethical data practices. This involves considering the human impact of data handling decisions and prioritizing the ethical treatment of user information.

Evolving Landscape: Adaptation to Technological Advances

As technology evolves, so must data protection and privacy policies. The advent of technologies like artificial intelligence, machine learning, and the Internet of Things introduces new challenges and considerations. Organizations need to adapt their policies to address the ethical and privacy implications of these emerging technologies, ensuring that users are protected in a landscape of continuous innovation.

Corporate Responsibility: Fostering a Culture of Privacy

Fostering a culture of privacy is not solely a regulatory requirement; it is a demonstration of corporate responsibility. Organizations that prioritize privacy as a core value contribute to building trust with their user base. This commitment goes beyond legal obligations to encompass ethical considerations, transparency, and a genuine respect for the privacy rights of individuals.

MANAGING AND RESPONDING TO PRIVACY INCIDENTS

In the digital age, where personal information is the currency of the online realm, the management and response to privacy incidents have become critical components of responsible data handling. Privacy incidents encompass a spectrum of events, from data breaches to unauthorized access that pose risks to the confidentiality, integrity, and availability of personal data. This exploration delves into the human-centric aspects of managing and responding to privacy incidents, shedding light on the importance of swift, transparent, and empathetic actions in the face of these challenges.

The Anatomy of Privacy Incidents: Unraveling the Complexity

Privacy incidents come in various forms, each with its own set of complexities. The most common among them is a data breach, where unauthorized access or disclosure of sensitive information occurs. This could involve personal data such as names, addresses, financial details, or even more intimate details, depending on the nature of the data held by an organization. Other incidents may include accidental data exposure, insider threats, or the compromise of systems hosting personal information. Understanding the nuances of these incidents is crucial for effective management and response.

The Human Impact: Beyond the Technicalities

Behind every privacy incident lies a human story—a person whose personal information has been exposed, a customer whose trust has been shaken, or an employee grappling with the aftermath. Recognizing the human impact is a fundamental aspect of responding to privacy incidents. It involves empathy for those affected, an acknowledgment of the potential emotional distress, and a commitment to mitigating harm beyond the technical resolution of the incident.

The Importance of Preparedness: Building a Response Framework

Preparedness is the cornerstone of effective incident management. Organizations must proactively establish a robust response framework that outlines roles, responsibilities, and procedures for addressing privacy incidents. This includes having a designated incident response team, clear communication channels, and predefined steps for investigation, containment, eradication, recovery, and lessons learned. A well-prepared organization can navigate the turbulent waters of a privacy incident with agility and resilience.

The Clock is ticking: Swift Response is Paramount

In the aftermath of a privacy incident, time becomes a precious commodity. Swift response is paramount, not only to contain the incident and prevent further damage but also to demonstrate to affected individuals that their concerns are being addressed promptly. Delays in response can exacerbate the impact of the incident, erode trust, and expose organizations to legal and reputational consequences. Timeliness is, therefore, a measure of commitment to accountability and user-centricity.

Communication as a Pillar: Transparent and Empathetic Outreach

Communication is the bridge that connects organizations with the individuals affected by a privacy incident. Transparent and empathetic outreach is crucial during all stages of incident response. This involves promptly notifying affected parties, clearly explaining the nature of the incident, the data involved, and the steps being taken to address the situation. Transparent communication builds trust, while empathy acknowledges the potential distress experienced by those impacted.

Regulatory Obligations: Navigating the Legal Landscape

Privacy incidents trigger legal obligations, especially in jurisdictions with robust data protection laws. Organizations must navigate this legal landscape with care, ensuring compliance with notification requirements, reporting obligations to regulatory authorities, and potential repercussions for non-compliance. Understanding the specific legal obligations applicable to the incident is vital for a comprehensive and compliant response.

The Human Face of Incident Response: Supporting Affected Individuals

Behind the legal and technical dimensions of incident response is a human face—the individuals whose personal information has been compromised. Supporting affected individuals involves more than just meeting legal requirements. It encompasses providing resources for identity protection, offering avenues for counseling or support, and demonstrating a commitment to alleviating the potential emotional toll of a privacy incident. In doing so, organizations move beyond compliance to truly address the well-being of those affected.

Forensic Investigation: Unraveling the How's and Whys

A thorough forensic investigation is a key component of incident response. This involves unraveling the intricacies of the incident—how it occurred, the extent of the compromise, and the potential vulnerabilities that were exploited. Forensic experts play a crucial role in piecing together this puzzle, providing organizations with insights to not only address the immediate incident but also fortify defenses against future threats.

Remediation and Strengthening Defenses: Learning from Incidents

Every privacy incident is an opportunity for learning and improvement. Remediation involves not only fixing the immediate issues but also strengthening overall cybersecurity defenses. This may include patching vulnerabilities, enhancing access controls, and fortifying systems to prevent similar incidents in the future. A proactive approach to learning from incidents contributes to organizational resilience and a continuous cycle of improvement.

Post-Incident Evaluation: A Critical Reflection

Once the incident is resolved, a post-incident evaluation is crucial. This involves reflecting on the entire incident response process, identifying strengths and weaknesses, and incorporating lessons learned into future incident response planning. This reflective process ensures that organizations evolve and adapt based on their experiences, fostering a culture of continuous improvement.

Rebuilding Trust: A Delicate Endeavor

Trust, once shaken by a privacy incident, is a delicate thing to rebuild. Organizations must invest in rebuilding trust through ongoing communication, transparency, and tangible actions that demonstrate a commitment to data protection. This may involve implementing additional security measures, offering enhanced privacy features, or engaging in community outreach initiatives to showcase a renewed dedication to user trust.

Cultural Shift: Embedding Privacy as a Core Value

Managing and responding to privacy incidents is not just a technical or legal endeavor; it requires a cultural shift within organizations. Embedding privacy as a core value involves fostering a mindset where every employee recognizes their role in safeguarding personal information. This cultural shift extends beyond incident response to influence day-to-day operations, product development, and decision-making at all levels of the organization.

Third-Party Collaboration: Strengthening the Ecosystem

In an interconnected digital ecosystem, incidents at one organization can have ripple effects on others. Collaboration with third parties, including vendors, partners, and industry peers, strengthens the overall resilience of the ecosystem. Sharing threat intelligence, best practices, and lessons learned enhances the collective ability to respond to and mitigate the impact of privacy incidents.

The Human Element: Training and Awareness

The human element is both a vulnerability and a strength in the realm of privacy incidents. Training and awareness programs are crucial for empowering employees with the knowledge and skills to recognize and respond to potential threats. An informed and vigilant workforce acts as a frontline defense against incidents, contributing to a proactive and resilient organizational posture.

Continuous Monitoring: Anticipating and Mitigating Future Threats

Privacy incidents are not isolated events; they are part of an ongoing landscape of cyber threats. Continuous monitoring involves actively anticipating and mitigating future threats. This may include the use of advanced threat detection tools, regular security assessments, and staying informed about emerging trends in cybersecurity. By adopting a proactive stance, organizations can reduce the likelihood and impact of future incidents.

Chapter 5

INFORMATION MANAGEMENT GUIDELINES

UNDERSTANDING INFORMATION MANAGEMENT

In an age where information flows seamlessly across networks and platforms, the concept of information management is an essential topic. At its essence, information management is not just technical jargon; it's a multifaceted approach to handling, organizing, and leveraging information in a manner that aligns with organizational goals and values. This exploration delves into the human-centric dimensions of understanding information management, shedding light on its significance, key principles, and the implications for individuals navigating the intricate web of the digital era.

Understanding the Essence of Information Management

At its core, information management is about making sense of the vast sea of data that surrounds us. It's about transforming raw data into meaningful insights, facilitating decision-making processes, and ensuring that information is not just stored but utilized effectively. Imagine a well- organized library where books are not only cataloged but also readily accessible, relevant, and contribute to a greater body of knowledge. Information management strives to create a similar order in the digital realm, where data is transformed into a valuable resource rather than an overwhelming burden.

The Multifaceted Nature of Information

Information is not a monolithic entity; it comes in various forms, each with its unique characteristics and relevance. From structured data stored in databases to unstructured content in documents and multimedia, information management encompasses the full spectrum. Understanding the multifaceted nature of information involves recognizing its diversity, context, and the different ways it can be harnessed to drive innovation, efficiency, and informed decision-making.

Key Principles of Information Management:

Several key principles underpin effective information management, weaving a tapestry of best practices that organizations strive to embrace:

Accessibility and Availability

Information should be accessible when needed and available to those who require it. This involves implementing systems and tools that facilitate easy retrieval without compromising security or integrity.

Data Quality

The adage "garbage in, garbage out" holds true in the realm of information management. Ensuring the quality of data, including accuracy, completeness, and consistency, is fundamental for reliable decision-making and analysis.

Security and Confidentiality

Information is a valuable asset, and safeguarding it against unauthorized access, breaches, and malicious activities is paramount. Balancing accessibility with security ensures that sensitive information remains confidential and protected.

Lifecycle Management

Information has a lifecycle, from creation and storage to archiving or disposal. Effective information management involves understanding and managing this lifecycle, ensuring that information is retained only as long as necessary and in compliance with regulatory requirements.

User Empowerment

Individuals interacting with information systems should be empowered to make the most of available resources. This involves providing training, user-friendly interfaces, and tools that enhance information literacy and user capabilities.

Integration and Interoperability

Information is often scattered across different systems and platforms. Integration and interoperability enable seamless communication between these systems, preventing data silos and fostering a holistic view of information.

Strategic Alignment

Information management should align with organizational goals and strategies. It's not just about managing data for its own sake but leveraging it strategically to drive business outcomes, innovation, and competitive advantage.

Implications for Individuals and Organizations

Understanding information management carries profound implications for both individuals and organizations immersed in the digital landscape:

Empowering Decision-Making

For individuals, information management empowers decision-making. Whether in personal or professional contexts, having access to relevant, accurate, and timely information enables informed choices and actions.

Enhancing Efficiency

Organizations benefit from streamlined operations and enhanced efficiency through effective information management. Accessible and well-organized information accelerates processes, reduces redundancy, and fosters collaboration.

Innovation Catalyst

The effective management of information serves as a catalyst for innovation. It allows organizations to harness data for insights, identify trends, and uncover opportunities for continuous improvement and strategic advancement.

Risk Mitigation

Recognizing the importance of security and confidentiality in information management is crucial for mitigating risks. Proactive measures to safeguard sensitive information protect individuals and organizations from the potentially damaging consequences of data breaches.

Adaptability in the Digital Era

In a rapidly evolving digital landscape, understanding information management is synonymous with adaptability. It involves staying abreast of technological advancements, embracing new tools and methodologies, and cultivating a culture of continuous learning.

Challenges in Information Management

While the principles of information management are clear, organizations often face challenges in implementation:

Data Overload

The sheer volume of data generated daily can be overwhelming. Navigating through this data deluge to extract meaningful insights without succumbing to information overload is a persistent challenge.

Data Silos

Information often resides in isolated silos within organizations, limiting its accessibility and usability. Breaking down these silos requires concerted efforts to integrate systems and promote collaboration.

Technological Complexity

The rapid pace of technological evolution introduces complexities in information management. Organizations must grapple with choosing and implementing technologies that align with their needs and can adapt to future changes.

Security Concerns

Balancing accessibility with security is an ongoing challenge. As organizations seek to make information readily available, they must concurrently implement robust security measures to safeguard against potential threats.

Compliance and Regulations

The landscape of data protection and privacy regulations is ever-changing. Navigating this complex terrain to ensure compliance adds another layer of challenge to information management efforts.

Strategies for Effective Information Management

To overcome these challenges and reap the benefits of effective information management, organizations can adopt several strategies:

Data Governance Framework

Implementing a robust data governance framework establishes accountability, ownership, and clear processes for information management. This involves defining roles, responsibilities, and policies governing data across the organization.

Advanced Analytics and AI

Leveraging advanced analytics and artificial intelligence (AI) capabilities can enhance information management. These technologies can sift through vast amounts of data, uncover patterns, and provide valuable insights for decision-making.

User-Centric Design

Designing information systems with a focus on user needs and experiences promotes user adoption and engagement. Intuitive interfaces, user-friendly tools, and personalized experiences contribute to effective information management.

Continuous Training and Education

Keeping individuals abreast of information management best practices through continuous training and education is crucial. This empowers users to navigate information systems effectively and make informed decisions.

Agile Information Architecture

Embracing an agile information architecture enables organizations to adapt to changing business needs. This involves designing systems that are flexible, scalable, and can accommodate new data sources and technologies.

INFORMATION CLASSIFICATION AND HANDLING

The concept of information classification and handling stands as a crucial pillar of responsible data management. At its core, this practice is not a mere technicality; it's a thoughtful and strategic approach to organizing, safeguarding, and utilizing information in a manner that aligns with organizational goals and values. This exploration aims to shed light on the human- centric dimensions of information classification and handling, unraveling the significance, key principles, and implications for individuals navigating the intricate web of the digital era.

Understanding Information Classification: Beyond Labels

Information classification is the process of categorizing data based on its sensitivity, importance, and confidentiality. This goes beyond attaching labels; it involves a nuanced understanding of the value and potential risks associated with different types of information. Imagine a library where books are not only shelved but also organized by genre, subject matter, and accessibility. Information classification seeks to create a similar structure in the digital realm, ensuring that data is treated according to its significance and the level of protection it requires.

The Spectrum of Sensitivity: Diverse Types of Information

Information comes in various forms, each with its own nuances and implications for handling:

Public Information

This includes data that is meant for public consumption, devoid of sensitive details. Public information can be freely shared and does not pose risks to individuals or organizations when disclosed.

Internal Use Only

Certain information is intended for internal use within an organization. While not classified as highly sensitive, it carries a level of confidentiality that merits controlled access and responsible handling.

Confidential Information

This category encompasses sensitive data that requires a higher level of protection. Confidential information may include trade secrets, financial data, or personally identifiable information (PII) that, if exposed, could lead to adverse consequences.

Restricted or Classified Information

In certain contexts, particularly in government or defense sectors, information may be classified based on its potential impact on national security. This level of information requires the strictest controls and is accessible only to authorized personnel.

Key Principles of Information Handling

Effectively handling information involves adhering to key principles that guide responsible and secure practices:

Need-to-Know Basis

Access to information should be granted on a need-to- know basis. Individuals should only have access to the data required for their specific roles or responsibilities, minimizing the risk of unauthorized exposure.

Access Controls

Implementing robust access controls ensures that information is only accessible by authorized personnel. This involves user authentication, encryption, and other measures to prevent unauthorized entry.

Encryption

Utilizing encryption techniques adds an additional layer of security to sensitive information. Encrypting data in transit and at rest safeguards it from interception or unauthorized access.

Regular Audits and Monitoring

Conducting regular audits and monitoring activities help identify any unusual or unauthorized access to information. This proactive approach enables organizations to address potential breaches promptly.

Secure Transmission

When information needs to be transmitted, employing secure channels such as Virtual Private Networks (VPNs) or secure email systems ensures that data is not intercepted or compromised during transit.

Disposal Procedures

Information has a lifecycle, and secure disposal procedures are essential. When data is no longer needed, proper deletion or destruction measures should be in place to prevent inadvertent exposure.

User Awareness and Training

Building awareness among users about the importance of information handling and providing training on secure practices contribute to a culture of responsibility and vigilance.

Implications for Individuals and Organizations

Understanding information classification and handling carries profound implications for both individuals and organizations navigating the digital landscape:

Trust and Reputation

For organizations, responsible information handling is intricately tied to trust and reputation. Mishandling sensitive information can erode trust among customers, clients, and partners, potentially causing lasting damage to an organization's reputation.

Legal Compliance

Adhering to information handling principles is crucial for legal compliance, especially in the context of data protection and privacy regulations. Violations can result in legal consequences and financial penalties.

Employee Morale

Individuals within organizations benefit from a sense of security knowing that their data is handled responsibly. This contributes to a positive work environment and employee morale.

Innovation and Collaboration

Secure information handling fosters an environment conducive to innovation and collaboration. When individuals trust that their ideas and contributions are protected, they are more likely to engage in collaborative efforts without fear of compromise.

Data-driven Decision-Making

Organizations rely on data for decision-making. Effective information handling ensures that the data used for analysis and decision-making is accurate, reliable, and representative of the organization's reality.

Challenges in Information Classification and Handling

Despite the principles and benefits, organizations often encounter challenges in effectively implementing information classification and handling practices:

Complexity of Data

The sheer complexity of data, especially in large organizations, makes it challenging to accurately classify and manage every piece of information.

Human Error

Employees may inadvertently mishandle information due to human error. This could involve sharing sensitive data with the wrong recipients or neglecting proper disposal procedures.

Balancing Security and Accessibility

Striking the right balance between securing sensitive information and ensuring accessibility for authorized users can be a delicate challenge.

Technological Advancements

The rapid pace of technological advancements introduces new complexities. Organizations must continually adapt their information handling practices to align with emerging technologies.

Cost Considerations

Implementing robust information handling practices often requires investments in technology, training, and ongoing monitoring. Balancing these costs with the benefits can be a strategic challenge for organizations.

Strategies for Effective Information Classification and Handling

To address these challenges and enhance information classification and handling, organizations can adopt several strategies:

Clear Policies and Guidelines

Establishing clear and comprehensive policies and guidelines for information classification and handling provides a foundation for organizational practices.

Technology Solutions

Utilize technology solutions such as data loss prevention (DLP) tools, encryption software, and secure collaboration platforms to enhance information security.

Training Programs

Implement regular training programs to educate employees about the importance of information classification and handling. This includes raising awareness about potential risks and best practices.

Incident Response Plans

Develop robust incident response plans to address potential breaches promptly and effectively. This involves having protocols in place for investigation, containment, and communication in the event of a security incident.

Cross-functional Collaboration

Foster collaboration between IT, security teams, legal departments, and end-users. A cross-functional approach ensures that information handling practices align with legal requirements, technical capabilities, and user needs.

SECURE FILE TRANSFER AND STORAGE

In the fast-paced, interconnected digital landscape, the need for secure file transfer and storage has become paramount. This isn't just a concern for tech-savvy professionals; it's a fundamental consideration for anyone who interacts with digital information, be it personal photos or sensitive business documents. Let's delve into the human side of this tech-savvy world, understanding why secure file transfer and storage matter, the challenges we face, and practical strategies for safeguarding our digital assets.

The Significance of Secure File Transfer and Storage:

Imagine the digital realm as a bustling marketplace, with information flowing like a vibrant stream. In this bustling environment, your files are like precious goods— some are valuable assets, and others are deeply personal. Secure file transfer and storage act as the guardians of this digital marketplace, ensuring that your valuable goods reach their intended recipients unscathed and that they are stored safely for future use.

Protecting Valuables in Transit

When you send a file to a friend, upload a document to the cloud, or share a project with colleagues, it's akin to dispatching a valuable package. Secure file transfer ensures that this package travels securely through the digital highways, shielding it from prying eyes or potential threats.

Preserving Digital Memories

Think of your family photos or personal documents as cherished memories stored in a digital treasure chest. Secure storage safeguards these memories, preventing accidental loss, unauthorized access, or the devastating impact of cyber threats that could erase your digital history.

Safeguarding Business Assets

For businesses, proprietary information, client data, and intellectual property are the lifeblood of operations. Secure file transfer and storage become the fortress protecting this vital information, ensuring that it remains confidential and intact amid the constant ebb and flow of digital transactions.

Challenges We Encounter

The digital marketplace, like any bustling bazaar, has its share of challenges. Understanding these challenges is crucial for navigating the intricate paths of secure file transfer and storage:

Cyber Threats and Hackers

In the bustling digital marketplace, cyber threats and hackers are the pickpockets and tricksters. They lurk in the shadows, attempting to compromise the confidentiality and integrity of your files during transit or storage.

Human Error

Just as misplacing a physical item is a common occurrence, so is accidentally sending a file to the wrong recipient or deleting important information. Human error poses a significant challenge to the security of our digital valuables.

Interoperability Concerns

In our diverse digital marketplace, not all systems speak the same language. Interoperability concerns arise when transferring files between different platforms or applications, potentially leading to data corruption or loss.

Compliance and Regulation

Imagine navigating a bustling market with ever- changing rules. In the digital realm, compliance and regulations add complexity. Adhering to data protection laws, industry standards, and organizational policies becomes a balancing act in the face of evolving regulations.

Practical Strategies for Secure File Transfer and Storage

In this dynamic digital marketplace, where the stakes are high and the challenges diverse, adopting practical strategies can fortify your approach to secure file transfer and storage:

Encryption: The Digital Lockbox

Encryption is like placing your valuables in a digital lockbox. It scrambles your files into unreadable code during transfer or storage, ensuring that even if intercepted, they remain indecipherable to unauthorized eyes.

Secure File Transfer Protocols

Think of file transfer protocols as trustworthy couriers in the digital marketplace. Protocols like SFTP (Secure File Transfer Protocol) or HTTPS (Hypertext Transfer Protocol Secure) provide encrypted pathways, adding an extra layer of protection to your digital packages during transit.

Multi-Factor Authentication (MFA): Extra Keys to the Vault

Just as a vault requires multiple keys for access, multi-factor authentication adds an extra layer of security to your digital vault. Whether accessing files or logging into storage platforms, MFA ensures that only authorized individuals have the keys to your digital treasures.

Regular Backups: A Safety Deposit Box for Digital Assets

Regular backups are like storing copies of your valuables in a safety deposit box. In the event of accidental loss, corruption, or cyber threats, backups act as a fail-safe, allowing you to restore your digital assets to a previous, secure state.

User Education and Vigilance

Just as you'd stay vigilant in a crowded marketplace, fostering user education and awareness is key. Educate users about the importance of secure practices, avoiding suspicious links, and verifying recipients before sending sensitive files.

Secure Cloud Storage: The Digital Warehouse

Secure cloud storage is akin to a fortified digital warehouse. Choosing reputable cloud providers with robust security measures ensures that your files are stored in a resilient environment protected from both physical and cyber threats.

Data Classification and Access Controls: Restricting Entry to Authorized Guests

Classify your digital valuables based on their sensitivity and implement access controls. Just as you wouldn't let everyone into your private space, restricting access ensures that only authorized individuals can interact with specific files.

Compliance Management

Stay informed about the rules governing the digital marketplace. Regularly update your understanding of data protection regulations, industry compliance standards, and organizational policies to ensure that your practices align with the ever-evolving landscape.

UNDERSTANDING THE IMPORTANCE OF INFORMATION MANAGEMENT

In the vast expanse of the digital age, where information flows like a river, understanding the importance of information management is akin to navigating the currents of a powerful stream. Information, the lifeblood of our interconnected world, is both a valuable asset and a potential source of overwhelm. In this exploration, let's unravel the human-centric dimensions of why information management matters, transcending the technicalities to grasp its significance in our daily lives.

The Digital Onslaught: Navigating the Information Deluge

Imagine the digital realm as a bustling marketplace, with information vendors vying for attention. In this bustling marketplace, we encounter a constant deluge of data—emails, documents, photos, and a myriad of digital artifacts. The sheer volume of information can be overwhelming, akin to traversing a crowded market where every vendor is clamoring for your attention. Without effective information management, it's like wading through this marketplace without a map, struggling to find what's essential amidst the noise.

Empowering Decision-Making: The Beacon in the Data Storm

At its core, information management is the beacon that guides us through the storm of data. It's about transforming raw data into meaningful insights, offering a compass for decision-making in both personal and professional realms. In our bustling digital marketplace, decisions abound—what product to buy, which job offer to accept, or how to invest our time. Effective information management ensures that we can make informed choices, leveraging the wealth of available data to navigate our personal and professional journeys.

Preserving Digital Order in the Chaos: From Files to Memories

Consider your digital life as a collection of files, much like items in a market stall. From important work documents to cherished family photos, these digital artifacts form the fabric of our digital existence. Without information management, chaos ensues. Files become scattered, difficult to find, and the memories they represent risk fading into the digital ether. Information management is the caretaker of this digital order, ensuring that each file finds its rightful place, preserving the memories embedded within.

Efficiency in the Digital Bazaar: Streamlining Operations

In the bustling digital bazaar, where businesses operate along-side personal interactions, efficiency is paramount. Information management streamlines operations, ensuring that data flows seamlessly through the digital marketplace. It's the architect designing the pathways that connect vendors, customers, and stakeholders. Whether it's optimizing supply chains, streamlining communication, or enhancing collaboration, effective information management is the backbone of operational efficiency in our interconnected world.

Guardianship of Sensitive Treasures: Privacy and Security

Imagine your personal information as a treasured possession in the digital marketplace. From financial details to intimate conversations, these are treasures that demand safeguarding. Information management is the guardian, standing watch to ensure the security and privacy of your digital valuables. In a world where cyber threats lurk like shadows in a crowded market, effective information management becomes the digital shield, protecting your sensitive treasures from unauthorized eyes and malicious actors.

The Symphony of Collaboration: Harmonizing Human Interaction

Our digital interactions are like a symphony in the bustling marketplace. Whether collaborating on projects or connecting with friends and colleagues, effective information management harmonizes these human interactions. It provides the sheet music that guides the musicians, ensuring that the collective efforts of individuals contribute to a beautiful symphony rather than a cacophony of discordant notes. In a world where collaboration spans geographical boundaries, information management becomes the conductor orchestrating the collaborative endeavors of individuals.

Innovation as a Tapestry: Weaving Insights and Ideas

In the crowded digital marketplace, innovation is the colorful tapestry woven from insights and ideas. Information management is the loom that facilitates this weaving process. By organizing and synthesizing data, information management enables individuals and organizations to uncover patterns, identify opportunities, and innovate. It's the catalyst that transforms the raw material of information into the fabric of innovation, driving progress and evolution in our interconnected world.

A Balancing Act: Privacy, Compliance, and Ethics

As we navigate the bustling digital bazaar, a delicate balancing act unfolds. Privacy, compliance with regulations, and ethical considerations become integral parts of the dance. Information management is the navigator, guiding individuals and organizations through the complex terrain of data protection laws, industry regulations, and ethical considerations. It ensures that in our pursuit of knowledge and progress, we tread responsibly and ethically through the digital marketplace.

Navigating the Waves of Change: Adaptability in the Digital Ocean

In the dynamic digital ocean, where waves of change are constant, information management is the vessel that allows us to navigate and adapt. It's the sail that catches the winds of technological advancements, steering us through the currents of evolving platforms and tools. Without effective information management, we risk being adrift in the digital ocean, unable to harness the trans-formative power of change for our benefit.

IDENTIFYING SENSITIVE DATA AND HOW TO PROTECT IT

In the vast digital landscape where information flows freely, iden-tifying sensitive data is akin to recognizing the hidden treasures within a bustling marketplace. From personal details to critical business information, sensitive data represents valuable assets that require careful protection. In this exploration, we'll unravel the human-centric process of identifying sensitive data and prac-tical strategies to safeguard these digital treasures, steering clear of technical jargon to make the journey relatable and accessible.

Unveiling the Digital Treasures: What is Sensitive Data?

Sensitive data encompasses a spectrum of information that, if exposed or mishandled, could lead to adverse consequences. Think of it as the assortment of treasures you safeguard in your home—analogous to your financial records, health information, or personally identifiable details. For businesses, sensitive data extends to proprietary information, trade secrets, and client data. Recognizing the value and potential risks associated with these digital treasures is the first step in their protection.

Personal Information

Your personal details, such as name, address, social security number, or medical records, are akin to the treasures in your personal vault. If these details fall into the wrong hands, they can be exploited for identity theft or financial fraud.

Financial Data

Think of your financial records as the currency in the digital marketplace. Bank account numbers, credit card details, and transaction history are valuable targets for cybercriminals seeking unauthorized access or fraudulent activities.

Intellectual Property

For businesses, intellectual property represents a unique set of treasures. This includes trade secrets, product designs, or proprietary algorithms—information that, if exposed, could undermine competitive advantages and innovation.

Client and Employee Information

In the business realm, client and employee data are critical treasures. This includes names, contact details, and, in some cases, sensitive information such as medical records or performance evaluations. Mishandling this data not only jeopardizes individuals' privacy but also erodes trust in the organization.

The Human Element: Recognizing Sensitivity

Identifying sensitive data is not solely a technical endeavor—it involves a nuanced understanding of the human element. Imagine sifting through your belongings at home; certain items hold sentimental value or require special care. Similarly, recognizing sensitivity in digital data requires an awareness of context, cultural nuances, and an understanding of the potential impact on individuals or organizations.

Cultural Sensitivity

What might be considered sensitive in one cultural context may differ in another. Understanding cultural nuances is crucial. For example, health information that is sensitive in one culture may be openly discussed in another.

Contextual Awareness

Recognizing sensitivity requires understanding the context in which data is used. A simple email address may not be inherently sensitive, but in the context of a healthcare platform, it becomes a piece of personally identifiable information.

Individual Perspectives

Sensitivity is often subjective. A customer complaint lodged on a public forum might be sensitive to a company's reputation. Recognizing the perspectives of individuals involved is essential in identifying and protecting sensitive data.

Practical Strategies for Safeguarding Digital Treasures:

Once sensitive data is identified, the next crucial step is safeguarding these digital treasures. Let's explore practical strategies that anyone, whether an individual or a business professional, can employ to protect sensitive data in the digital landscape.

Encryption: Securing the Vault

Imagine your sensitive data as treasures stored in a vault. Encryption is the digital lock that ensures even if someone gains access, the contents remain indecipherable. Applying encryption to sensitive files, emails, or communications adds an extra layer of security, turning your digital vault into an impregnable fortress.

Access Controls: Restricting Entry

Just as you wouldn't grant access to your personal vault to just anyone, controlling who can access sensitive data is critical. Implementing access controls ensures that only authorized individuals have the keys to your digital treasures. This can involve password protection, multi-factor authentication, or role-based access, tailoring permissions based on responsibilities.

Regular Audits: Taking Inventory

Imagine periodically taking inventory of your physical valuables to ensure nothing is missing or misplaced. Regular audits of digital data serve a similar purpose. Conducting audits helps identify any unusual or unauthorized access to sensitive data, enabling timely intervention and correction.

Secure Communication Channels: Trusted Couriers

When sending or receiving sensitive information, think of communication channels as trusted couriers. Utilizing secure protocols like HTTPS for websites, or encrypted email services, ensures that your digital packages traverse the digital highways with minimal risk of interception or compromise.

Data Classification: Labeling Your Treasures

In the digital realm, data classification is akin to labeling your treasures. It involves categorizing data based on its sensitivity and applying appropriate protection measures. This ensures that everyone interacting with the data understands its importance and handles it accordingly.

Employee Training: Empowering Guardians

Just as you'd educate family members about the importance of safeguarding valuables, employee training is crucial in the business realm. Empowering individuals with the knowledge and skills to recognize, handle, and protect sensitive data turns them into guardians of digital treasures.

Incident Response Plans: Emergency Protocols

Consider incident response plans as emergency protocols for your digital treasures. In case of a security breach or unauthorized access, having a well-defined plan ensures swift and effective responses, minimizing the potential impact on sensitive data.

Secure Cloud Storage: The Fortified Vault

For individuals and businesses alike, secure cloud storage serves as the fortified vault for digital treasures. Choosing reputable cloud service providers with robust security measures ensures that your sensitive data is stored in a resilient environment, protected from both physical and cyber threats.

The Human Touch in Protection: Ethical Considerations

Protecting sensitive data goes beyond technical measures—it involves ethical considerations. Imagine being entrusted with someone else's valuables; respecting their privacy and safeguarding their trust becomes paramount. This ethical dimension includes transparency in data handling, obtaining consent, and ensuring that the protection measures align with legal and ethical standards.

DEVELOPING POLICIES AND PROCEDURES FOR MANAGING INFORMATION

In the dynamic and interconnected landscape of the digital age, developing policies and procedures for managing information is akin to crafting a set of guiding principles for navigating a bustling city. Much like traffic rules and city ordinances maintain order and protect citizens, information management policies and procedures establish a framework for handling data responsibly and securely. In this exploration, let's unravel the human-centric aspects of why such policies are crucial, how they are developed, and the practical implications for individuals and organizations, steering clear of technical jargon to make the journey relatable and accessible.

The Urban Landscape of Information: Why Policies Matter

Imagine the vast expanse of information as a sprawling city, with data flowing through digital streets like the hustle and bustle of daily life. In this cityscape, policies and procedures act as the urban planning guidelines, shaping the infrastructure and ensuring that the city functions harmoniously. Similarly, in the digital realm, information management policies play a pivotal role in maintaining order, protecting sensitive data, and fostering a culture of responsibility.

Trust and Reputation

Just as a well-planned city fosters trust among its residents, information management policies contribute to the trust and reputation of individuals and organizations. Users, whether employees or customers, want assurance that their data is handled responsibly. Effective policies build this assurance, cultivating a positive reputation in the digital landscape.

Compliance with Regulations

The digital city has its own set of laws and regulations governing data protection and privacy. Information management policies act as a legal guide, ensuring that individuals and organizations adhere to these regulations. From GDPR to HIPAA, policies help navigate the complex legal terrain, preventing legal repercussions and safeguarding against penalties.

Efficiency in Operations

In a well-organized city, traffic flows smoothly, and services are delivered efficiently. Similarly, information management policies streamline operations in the digital realm. By providing guidelines on data storage, retrieval, and sharing, policies enhance the efficiency of information processes, preventing bottlenecks and ensuring the seamless flow of data.

Security and Privacy

Picture well-lit streets and secure neighborhoods in a city—information management policies create a similar environment for digital data. By outlining security measures, encryption protocols, and privacy controls, policies act as the guardians of digital security, protecting sensitive information from unauthorized access and cyber threats.

Crafting the Blueprint: How Policies and Procedures are developed

Developing information management policies is a thoughtful process, much like designing the blueprint for a city's infrastructure. It involves collaboration, foresight, and a keen understanding of the needs and values of the community. Here's a human-centric view of how these policies are crafted:

Identifying Stakeholders

In city planning, involving community members ensures that diverse perspectives are considered. Similarly, in developing information management policies, stakeholders from various departments—IT, legal, compliance, and end- users—are brought together. This collaborative approach ensures that the policies are comprehensive and reflective of the organization's collective needs.

Understanding Organizational Goals

Just as a city's infrastructure aligns with its vision for development, information management policies should align with organizational goals. Whether its innovation, customer service, or regulatory compliance, policies are crafted to support and enhance these overarching objectives.

Risk Assessment

Every city faces unique risks, from natural disasters to economic challenges. Similarly, in the digital landscape, policies are developed after a thorough risk assessment. This involves identifying potential threats to information security, evaluating their impact, and devising measures to mitigate these risks.

User Involvement and Training

In a well-functioning city, residents are educated about local rules and encouraged to participate in community initiatives.

Similarly, involving end-users in the development of information management policies is crucial. User input ensures that policies are practical, user-friendly, and aligned with the day-to-day realities of those interacting with data.

Legal Compliance

City ordinances are shaped by state and federal laws. Similarly, information management policies are developed with legal compliance in mind. Legal experts collaborate with policy developers to ensure that the policies align with data protection laws, industry regulations, and organizational obligations.

Communication and Transparency

Just as a city communicates new policies to its residents, organizations communicate information management policies to their employees. Transparent communication is key, providing clarity on the purpose of policies, the responsibilities of individuals, and the implications of non-compliance.

Practical Implications: Navigating the Digital City

Once the policies and procedures are in place, their practical implications become evident in the day-to-day functioning of the digital city. Let's explore these implications from a human-centric perspective:

User Empowerment

Well-crafted policies empower users to navigate the digital landscape confidently. Clear guidelines on data handling, secure communication practices, and privacy controls empower individuals to be responsible stewards of digital information.

Risk Mitigation

In the ever-evolving digital city, risks are inevitable. However, information management policies serve as a resilient shield, mitigating risks by providing a structured response to potential threats. Whether it's a data breach or a cybersecurity incident, policies guide organizations in effective risk management.

Cultural Shift

Just as city planning can contribute to a cultural shift, information management policies foster a culture of responsibility and accountability. When individuals understand the importance of data protection and their role in it, a positive cultural shift occurs, permeating the organization's ethos.

Continuous Improvement

A well-planned city adapts to changing needs and technological advancements. Similarly, information management policies are not static. Regular reviews, updates, and adjustments ensure that policies evolve to address new challenges and leverage emerging technologies for the benefit of the organization.

Privacy and Ethical Considerations

Ethical considerations are at the heart of a thriving city. Information management policies incorporate privacy and ethical guidelines, emphasizing the responsible and ethical use of data. This ensures that the organization operates with integrity, respecting the rights and privacy of individuals.

BEST PRACTICES FOR DATA BACKUP AND DISASTER RECOVERY

In the ever-evolving digital landscape, where data is the lifeblood of personal and professional endeavors, adopting best practices for data backup and disaster recovery is akin to having a reliable insurance policy for the unexpected. Imagine it as a safety net that ensures your digital assets remain intact, whether you face a hardware failure, a cyberattack, or a natural disaster. In this exploration, let's delve into the human side of these practices, understanding why they matter, how they are implemented, and the peace of mind they provide, all while avoiding technical jargon.

The Digital Chronicles: Why Backup and Recovery Matter

Consider your digital life as a collection of stories, each document, photo, or project representing a chapter. Now, imagine losing a chapter or even the entire book due to a hardware malfunction, a malicious attack, or an unforeseen disaster. The emotional toll of such a loss is profound. Best practices for data backup and disaster recovery emerge as the guardians of these digital chronicles, ensuring that your stories remain intact, ready to be revisited even in the face of adversity.

Preserving Memories

Your digital photos, videos, and documents are more than just files—they are memories encapsulated in pixels and bytes. Best practices for backup and recovery ensure that these memories are preserved. Losing a precious photo album or important document due to a technical glitch is akin to misplacing a cherished family heirloom. By adopting best practices, you safeguard these digital treasures, allowing you to revisit and share them for generations to come.

Protecting Productivity

In the professional realm, your projects, reports, and collaborative efforts are the heartbeat of productivity. Imagine investing hours or even months into a project only to lose it in an instant. Best practices for backup and recovery act as the safety net for productivity, ensuring that your hard work is not erased by a sudden hardware failure, a cyber- incident, or any unforeseen calamity.

Mitigating the Impact of Cyber Threats

The digital landscape is not without its shadows, with cyber threats lurking like unseen adversaries. Ransomware attacks, phishing attempts, and malicious software can encrypt or compromise your data. Best practices for backup and recovery offer a shield against such threats. If your data is compromised, you can restore it to a pre-attack state, minimizing the impact on your digital life.

Implementing Best Practices: A Human- Centric Approach

Now that we understand the emotional and practical importance of data backup and disaster recovery, let's explore how these best practices are implemented in a human-centric manner:

Regular Backups: Capturing the Essence of Your Digital Story

Think of regular backups as capturing the essence of your digital story at different points in time. This involves routinely copying and storing your data in a separate location, whether it's an external hard drive, a dedicated server, or a cloud-based service. Regularity is key; set up automated backups to ensure that your most recent chapters are always captured.

Choosing the Right Backup Storage: Your Digital Safe Deposit Box

Selecting the right storage for backups is akin to choosing a secure safe deposit box for your valuables. Cloud- based services, external hard drives, or network-attached storage (NAS) devices serve as your digital safe deposit boxes. Evaluate the options based on your needs, considering factors such as accessibility, capacity, and security.

Versioning: Preserving Multiple Drafts of Your Digital Work

Imagine being able to access different drafts of your work, each representing a different phase of your creative process. Versioning in backup practices allows you to do just that. It retains multiple versions of a file, enabling you to roll back to a specific point in time. This feature is especially valuable when unintended changes or errors occur.

Encryption: Locking Your Digital Safe

Consider encryption as the lock on your digital safe deposit box. It scrambles your data into unreadable code, ensuring that even if unauthorized access occurs, the content remains indecipherable. Encryption is an essential layer of security for both stored and transmitted data, protecting your digital valuables from prying eyes.

Testing Recovery Processes: Fire Drills for Your Digital Assets

Just as fire drills ensure preparedness in case of a real emergency, testing recovery processes is the digital equivalent. Regularly simulate the restoration of data from backups to ensure that the process is seamless and that your data is recoverable. This proactive approach guarantees that your safety net is intact and ready to deploy when needed.

Offsite Backup: Diversifying Your Digital Assets

Imagine diversifying your financial portfolio to mitigate risks. Offsite backups follow a similar principle. Storing backups in a different physical location or in the cloud ensures redundancy. In the event of a localized disaster, like a fire or flood, your offsite backup remains unaffected, allowing you to recover your data even if the primary location is compromised.

User Education: Empowering the Guardians of Data

Just as you'd educate someone on how to use a physical safe, user education is crucial for effective data backup and recovery. Empower individuals with the knowledge of how to initiate backups, understand recovery processes, and recognize the importance of these practices in preserving their digital assets.

The Peace of Mind: A Human Perspective on Security

Beyond the technicalities, the true essence of best practices for data backup and disaster recovery lies in the peace of mind they provide. Picture this peace of mind as a serene mental landscape where you know that, regardless of what digital storms may come, your data is shielded and can be restored. This peace of mind is rooted in the assurance that your digital stories, memories, and work are resilient in the face of unforeseen challenges.

Chapter 6

PHYSICAL SECURITY

OVERVIEW OF PHYSICAL SECURITY

Physical security serves as the tangible fortress that protects against real-world threats. Imagine it as the guardian at the gate, standing watch over the physical premises and resources, much like a vigilant sentinel. In this exploration, we'll unravel the human-centric dimensions of physical security—why it matters, how it is implemented, and the peace of mind it offers, all while avoiding technical jargon.

The Sentinel's Duty: Why Physical Security Matters

Picture your home, a sanctuary where you and your loved ones reside. Now, consider the importance of knowing that your home is secure, shielded from unauthorized access and potential dangers. Physical security extends this sense of assurance to various environments, from residential spaces to commercial establishments, critical infrastructure, and public spaces. At its core, physical security is about creating a safe and protected environment in the physical realm.

Personal Safety

Just as you'd lock your doors at night for personal safety, physical security ensures the safety of individuals within a given space. It encompasses measures to prevent unauthorized access, deter criminal activities, and respond effectively to emergencies, fostering an environment where people can live, work, and interact without fear.

Asset Protection

Consider the valuables within your home—the sentimental items, important documents, and possessions that hold personal significance. Physical security safeguards assets in a similar manner. In a business context, this could include protecting equipment, inventory, intellectual property, and other critical assets that contribute to the organization's well-being.

Preventing Unauthorized Access

Think of physical security as the gatekeeper, ensuring that only authorized individuals gain access to a designated area. Whether it's a secure facility, a data center, or a government building, controlling access is vital for maintaining the integrity and confidentiality of the space.

Deterrence of Criminal Activities

The presence of visible security measures acts as a deterrent to potential wrongdoers. It's the equivalent of having a well-lit street or a neighborhood watch program. Physical security measures send a clear message that unlawful activities will not go unnoticed, dissuading individuals with malicious intent.

Emergency Preparedness

Beyond deterring threats, physical security involves preparedness for emergencies. This could range from natural disasters like earthquakes and floods to human-made crises such as fires or security incidents. Having robust physical security measures in place ensures a swift and organized response to such unforeseen events.

Implementing Physical Security: A Human- Centric Approach

Understanding the human-centric approach to implementing physical security involves envisioning it as a set of practices and measures that resonate with our everyday experiences. These include the following.

Access Control: Securing the Gates

Imagine access control as the guardian at the gate of a medieval castle. It regulates who can enter, exit, and move within the fortress. In the modern context, access control involves mechanisms such as key cards, biometric scanners, or security personnel to manage and monitor access points. This ensures that only authorized individuals can enter specific areas, reinforcing the concept of personal space and privacy.

Surveillance: The Watchful Eye

Consider surveillance as the watchful eye that oversees a bustling marketplace. In physical security, surveillance involves the use of cameras and monitoring systems to observe and record activities. This not only acts as a deterrent but also provides a means to review incidents, investigate wrongdoing, and ensure the overall safety and security of a space.

Perimeter Security: Defining Boundaries

Think of perimeter security as the fences or walls that define the boundaries of a property. Whether it's a residential home, a commercial building, or a government facility, securing the perimeter is a fundamental aspect of physical security. It prevents unauthorized entry and sets the stage for a layered approach to security.

Security Personnel: Human Guardians

Imagine security personnel as the human guardians patrolling the streets of a neighborhood. In physical security, trained personnel play a crucial role in maintaining a visible presence, responding to incidents, and assisting with emergency situations. Their human touch brings a sense of reassurance to those within the secured space.

Emergency Response Plans: Preparedness for the Unexpected

Consider emergency response plans as akin to having a fire escape plan for your home. In physical security, these plans outline procedures for responding to various emergencies, from natural disasters to security incidents. This human-centric approach ensures that individuals within a space know what to do in critical situations, fostering a sense of preparedness and minimizing panic.

Environmental Design: Creating Safe Spaces

Think of environmental design as the thoughtful layout of a public park, with well-lit paths and clear signage. In physical security, designing spaces with safety in mind involves considerations such as adequate lighting, clear visibility, and strategic placement of security features. This approach contributes to the overall well-being and comfort of individuals within a given environment.

The Peace of Mind: A Human Perspective on Security

Beyond the physical measures, the essence of physical security lies in the peace of mind it offers. Picture this peace of mind as a tranquil haven within the bustling cityscape— knowing that the spaces you inhabit are secure, that your loved ones are protected, and that the physical environment is conducive to well-being. This peace of mind transcends mere surveillance cameras and access cards; it is rooted in the assurance that physical security measures create a sanctuary where individuals can thrive.

ACCESS CONTROL FOR PHYSICAL LOCATIONS

In the intricate dance between security and accessibility, access control for physical locations emerges as the choreographer, orchestrating the delicate balance between safeguarding and enabling. Imagine it as the maestro conducting the movements of a grand symphony, allowing authorized individuals to step into designated spaces while ensuring that unauthorized access remains a distant refrain. In this exploration, we'll unravel the human-centric dimensions of access control—why it matters, how it is implemented, and the impact it has on our daily experiences, all while avoiding technical jargon.

The Symphony of Security: Why Access Control Matters

Consider your home as a personal sanctuary. Now, envision the importance of knowing that only those you trust have the key to enter. Access control extends this principle to various physical locations, from residential spaces to corporate offices, educational institutions, and government facilities. At its core, access control is about managing who can enter a space, ensuring that it remains secure, and granting access only to those with legitimate reasons to be present.

Personal Safety

Just as you lock the doors of your home for personal safety, access control enhances safety in physical locations. It prevents unauthorized individuals from entering, creating a secure environment where people can live, work, and interact without the looming threat of unauthorized access.

Property Protection

Think of access control as the guardian of valuable possessions within your home. In a business context, this could include safeguarding assets such as equipment, inventory, sensitive information, and intellectual property. Access control ensures that only those with proper authorization can access these critical resources.

Confidentiality and Privacy:

Envision access control as a curtain drawn to protect the privacy of your personal space. In professional settings, access control safeguards confidential information and ensures that sensitive discussions remain within designated areas. This not only protects the privacy of individuals but also upholds the integrity of confidential business operations.

Regulating Traffic Flow

Picture access control as the traffic signals in a bustling city. It regulates the flow of people, allowing for smooth movement within a space. By managing entry points and exit routes, access control contributes to an organized and efficient environment, preventing overcrowding and ensuring orderly movement.

Implementing Access Control: A Human- Centric Approach

Understanding the human-centric approach to implementing access control involves envisioning it as a set of practices and measures that resonate with our everyday experiences:

Key Cards and Badges: Digital Passports

Imagine key cards and badges as the digital passports granting access to specific locations. In access control, these physical credentials serve as the means for individuals to prove their authorization. Swiping a key card or presenting a badge at an access point is akin to presenting a ticket to enter a concert venue—it grants permission based on the individual's credentials.

Biometric Recognition: Your Unique Signature

Think of biometric recognition as your unique signature that opens doors. Whether it's a fingerprint scan, facial recognition, or retina scan, biometrics identify individuals based on their unique physiological characteristics. This human-centric approach eliminates the need for physical keys or cards, relying on the distinctiveness of each person's biological features.

Visitor Management: Welcoming Guests

Consider visitor management as the concierge service for your space. In access control, this involves registering and monitoring visitors, providing them with temporary access credentials, and ensuring that their movements are supervised. This approach strikes a balance between hospitality and security, allowing for the controlled entry of guests.

Access Zones: Designated Areas

Imagine access zones as the different sections within a library—each requiring a specific level of authorization. In access control, different areas within a space may have varying access permissions. For example, only certain employees may have access to a server room or executive offices. This ensures that individuals can access only the areas relevant to their responsibilities.

Mobile Access: Digital Convenience

Think of mobile access as the digital key fob that resides in your smartphone. In this approach, individuals use their mobile devices as access credentials. This not only adds a layer of convenience but also aligns with the modern lifestyle, where smartphones serve as indispensable companions in daily activities.

The Impact on Daily Experiences: A Symphony of Effortless Security

Beyond the technicalities, the true essence of access control lies in the impact it has on our daily experiences. Picture this impact as the seamless melody of a well-played symphony—effortless, harmonious, and enriching:

Efficiency and Productivity

Access control streamlines entry and exit processes, contributing to the efficiency of daily operations. Individuals can move within a space without unnecessary delays, enhancing productivity and minimizing disruptions.

Employee Satisfaction

Access control ensures that employees have the access they need to perform their roles effectively. This contributes to job satisfaction, as individuals can navigate their workspaces without unnecessary barriers, fostering a positive work environment.

Safety and Well-Being

The security provided by access control enhances the overall safety and well-being of individuals within a space. Knowing that unauthorized access is mitigated creates a sense of security, allowing people to focus on their tasks without the constant concern of external threats.

Customized Experiences

Access control allows for customization based on roles and responsibilities. Whether it's granting access to specific floors, departments, or resources, individuals experience a tailored environment that aligns with their professional responsibilities.

Adaptability to Changing Needs

Access control is adaptable to evolving needs. As personnel changes occur or areas undergo modifications, access permissions can be easily adjusted. This adaptability ensures that access control remains aligned with the dynamic nature of organizations.

IMPLEMENTING SURVEILLANCE AND MONITORING

Implementing surveillance and monitoring is akin to having vigilant eyes that observe and record activities. Imagine it as a trusted guardian, standing watch over the surroundings, much like the attentive gaze of a caretaker. In this exploration, we'll delve into the human- centric dimensions of surveillance and monitoring—why they matter, how they are implemented, and the impact they have on our daily lives, all while avoiding technical jargon.

The Guardian's Watch: Why Surveillance and Monitoring Matter

Consider your neighborhood with its familiar streets and faces. Now, envision the importance of knowing that there is a watchful presence ensuring the safety of the community. Surveillance and monitoring extend this sense of assurance to various environments, from public spaces to private establishments, educational institutions, and beyond. At its core, surveillance and monitoring are about maintaining a watchful eye on activities, deterring potential threats, and providing a means to respond effectively to events.

Enhancing Safety

Just as you appreciate well-lit streets in your neighborhood, surveillance enhances safety in various environments. It acts as a deterrent to potential wrongdoers, creates a sense of visibility, and contributes to the overall security of a space. Knowing that activities are being observed fosters an environment where individuals feel safer and more secure.

Preventing Incidents

Imagine surveillance as the preemptive measure that prevents incidents before they occur. Whether it's deterring theft, monitoring for unauthorized access, or ensuring compliance with safety protocols, surveillance serves as a proactive tool to identify and address potential issues in real- time.

Providing Evidence

Consider surveillance as the impartial witness that records events without bias. In the event of an incident, surveillance footage provides valuable evidence for investigations. This not only aids in identifying individuals involved but also serves as an objective record of what transpired, facilitating a fair and accurate assessment.

Emergency Response

Think of surveillance as the communicator that relays information during emergencies. By monitoring activities, surveillance systems can detect anomalies or unusual patterns that may indicate a security threat or emergency. This early detection enables prompt response, contributing to effective emergency management.

Implementing Surveillance and Monitoring: A Human-Centric Approach

Understanding the human-centric approach to implementing surveillance and monitoring involves envisioning it as a set of practices and technologies that align with our everyday experiences:

Camera Systems: The Watchful Eyes

Imagine camera systems as the watchful eyes that capture the visual narrative of a space. These can include traditional closed-circuit television (CCTV) cameras, as well as more advanced and discreet surveillance technologies. The placement of cameras is strategic, covering key areas to ensure comprehensive coverage while respecting privacy considerations.

Remote Monitoring: The Virtual Guardian

Consider remote monitoring as the virtual guardian that oversees spaces from a distance. With advancements in technology, surveillance systems allow for remote access to live feeds and recorded footage. This flexibility not only enhances the efficiency of monitoring but also enables timely response to emerging situations, even from afar.

Smart Analytics: The Intelligent Observer

Think of smart analytics as the intelligent observer that sifts through vast amounts of data. Modern surveillance systems often incorporate artificial intelligence and analytics to detect anomalies, identify patterns, and even predict potential security threats. This intelligent processing adds a layer of efficiency to monitoring, reducing the need for constant human oversight.

Integration with Access Control: The Collaborative Duo

Imagine integration with access control as the collaborative duo that ensures comprehensive security. Surveillance systems can be integrated with access control measures, linking visual monitoring with data on who is entering or exiting a space. This synergy creates a more holistic approach to security, offering a layered defense against potential threats.

Privacy Considerations: The Ethical Guardian

Consider privacy considerations as the ethical guardian that balances security with individual rights. Implementing surveillance and monitoring involves respecting privacy norms and legal requirements. The deployment of surveillance systems should be accompanied by transparent communication about their purpose and adherence to privacy regulations.

The Impact on Daily Lives: A Symphony of Safety

Beyond the technicalities, the true essence of surveillance and monitoring lies in the impact they have on our daily lives. Picture this impact as the symphony of safety playing in the background—unseen yet present, contributing to the harmony of our shared spaces:

Peace of Mind

Surveillance and monitoring provide a sense of peace of mind, knowing that spaces are being actively observed. This assurance allows individuals to go about their daily activities without constant worry, fostering a positive and secure environment.

Community Well-Being

In communal spaces, surveillance contributes to the overall well-being of the community. It discourages anti- social behavior, prevents incidents that could affect the collective safety, and promotes a shared responsibility for maintaining a secure environment.

Quick Response to Incidents

The ability to monitor activities in real-time enables a swift response to emerging incidents. Whether it's a security threat or a safety concern, surveillance allows for timely intervention, minimizing the impact of incidents and ensuring the safety of those within the monitored space.

Accountability and Transparency

Surveillance fosters accountability and transparency. Knowing that activities are being recorded encourages responsible behavior, and in the event of incidents, the recorded footage provides an objective record. This contributes to a culture of transparency and fairness within a community or organization.

SECURING PHYSICAL ASSETS AND EQUIPMENT

Securing physical assets and equipment is akin to fortifying the stronghold that houses the lifeblood of an organization. Picture it as the guardian at the gate, standing watch over the tangible elements that propel productivity and contribute to the core functions of a business. In this exploration, we'll delve into the human-centric dimensions of securing physical assets and equipment—why it matters, how it is implemented, and the impact it has on the seamless flow of daily operations, all while avoiding technical jargon.

The Guardians of Productivity: Why Securing Physical Assets Matters

Consider a factory floor bustling with machines or an office filled with computers and specialized equipment. Now, envision the importance of knowing that these physical assets are protected, ensuring the gears of productivity continue to turn smoothly. Securing physical assets is about safeguarding the tools, machinery, technology, and other tangible elements that form the backbone of an organization.

Operational Continuity

Just as you secure your home to protect your belongings, securing physical assets ensures the uninterrupted flow of operations. Whether it's manufacturing equipment, computers, or specialized tools, the continuous operation of these assets is crucial for meeting production targets and sustaining business activities.

Preventing Loss and Theft

Imagine physical assets as the tools of a craft—each one holding intrinsic value. Securing these assets is about preventing loss or theft, which can have significant financial implications. Whether its inventory in a warehouse or specialized equipment in a research facility, the protection of these assets is vital for the financial health of an organization.

Preserving Intellectual Property

Think of securing physical assets as safeguarding the intellectual capital of an organization. In a world where innovation is a cornerstone of success, protecting proprietary technology, research equipment, and other intellectual assets becomes paramount. This not only preserves the organization's competitive edge but also upholds the integrity of its intellectual property.

Ensuring Workplace Safety

Consider securing physical assets as an essential aspect of ensuring workplace safety. Machinery, tools, and equipment need to be properly maintained and used to prevent accidents or injuries. Securing these assets involves implementing safety measures and protocols that contribute to a secure working environment.

Implementing Physical Asset Security: A Human-Centric Approach

Understanding the human-centric approach to implementing physical asset security involves envisioning it as a set of practices and measures that resonate with our everyday experiences:

Access Control: Safeguarding Entrances

Imagine access control as the gatekeeper at the entrance to a secure facility. In physical asset security, access control ensures that only authorized personnel can access areas where valuable assets are housed. This involves measures such as key cards, biometric access, or security personnel monitoring access points.

Surveillance and Monitoring: The Watchful Eyes

Consider surveillance and monitoring as the watchful eyes that oversee the spaces where physical assets are stored. Cameras and monitoring systems not only act as deterrents to potential theft or misuse but also provide a means to review incidents, investigate wrongdoing, and ensure the overall security of asset storage areas.

Inventory Management: Knowing What You Have

Think of inventory management as the meticulous cataloging of your belongings. In physical asset security, effective inventory management ensures that organizations know exactly what assets they possess, where they are located, and their current condition. This contributes to efficient maintenance and proactive measures to prevent loss or damage.

Asset Tagging: Digital Identification

Imagine asset tagging as the digital identification of each physical asset. This involves affixing unique identifiers or barcodes to assets, allowing for easy tracking and management. Asset tagging streamlines the process of monitoring the movement and usage of assets, reducing the risk of loss or misplacement.

Employee Training: Building a Security Culture

Consider employee training as the foundation of a security-conscious culture. Educating personnel on the importance of physical asset security, including proper usage, storage, and reporting procedures, creates a workforce that actively participates in maintaining a secure environment.

The Impact on Daily Operations: A Symphony of Seamless Workflows

Beyond the technicalities, the true essence of securing physical assets lies in the impact it has on daily operations. Picture this impact as the symphony of seamless workflows— each instrument playing its part in harmony, contributing to the overall efficiency of the organization:

Uninterrupted Operations

Securing physical assets ensures that operations remain uninterrupted. Whether it's the machinery on a production line, the computers in an office, or the specialized tools in a laboratory, the security measures in place contribute to the continuous flow of work.

Employee Confidence

Knowing that physical assets are secure fosters confidence among employees. This confidence translates into a sense of stability and trust in the workplace, allowing individuals to focus on their tasks without the distraction of concerns about the safety of the tools they rely on.

Resource Optimization

Effective physical asset security involves proactive maintenance and monitoring. This optimization of resources ensures that assets are in good working condition, minimizing downtime due to unexpected failures. It also contributes to the efficient allocation of resources, preventing unnecessary spending on replacements.

Risk Mitigation

Securing physical assets is a fundamental aspect of risk mitigation. By implementing access controls, surveillance, and inventory management, organizations reduce the risk of theft, loss, or damage to valuable assets. This proactive approach contributes to a lower likelihood of disruptive incidents.

Chapter 7

SOCIAL ENGINEERING

UNDERSTANDING SOCIAL ENGINEERING

Between technology and human interaction, social engineering emerges as a subtle yet potent force, transcending the realms of code and algorithms. Imagine it as the artful persuasion in the theater of human connection—a narrative woven not in lines of code but in the subtleties of communication. In this exploration, we'll delve into the human-centric dimensions of social engineering—what it is, how it operates, and the impact it has on our interconnected lives, all while avoiding technical jargon.

The Art of Persuasion: Understanding Social Engineering

At its essence, social engineering is the craft of manipulating individuals into divulging confidential information, granting access to secure systems, or performing actions that may compromise security. Unlike traditional cybersecurity threats that exploit technical vulnerabilities, social engineering exploits the inherent vulnerabilities of human psychology.

The Human Element

Picture the intricate dance of a masquerade ball—the interplay of personas, the artful disguises, and the subtle cues that reveal more than words convey. Social engineering recognizes the inherent human element in the security equation. It is not about breaching firewalls or exploiting software flaws; rather, it capitalizes on the intricacies of human behavior.

Psychological Manipulation

Imagine a masterful storyteller weaving a narrative that captivates the audience. Social engineering relies on psychological manipulation, using various tactics to influence individuals into taking actions they might not otherwise contemplate. This could range from exploiting trust to instilling fear or creating a false sense of urgency.

Diverse Techniques

Think of social engineering as a versatile performer on a stage, adapting its techniques to suit the context. It encompasses a spectrum of methods, including phishing emails, pretexting (creating a fabricated scenario to obtain information), impersonation, and baiting (luring individuals into a trap). Each technique is tailored to exploit different aspects of human psychology.

Exploiting Trust and Relationships

Consider social engineering as the subtle erosion of trust—a deceiving smile or a reassuring tone that masks malicious intent. Attackers often exploit existing relationships or impersonate trusted entities, leveraging the trust individuals place in familiar faces or authoritative figures to manipulate them into divulging sensitive information.

TYPES OF SOCIAL ENGINEERING ATTACKS

In the vast landscape of digital interactions, social engineering attacks unfold as a series of artful deceptions, exploiting the intricacies of human behavior rather than relying on technical vulnerabilities. Imagine it as a multifaceted performance on the stage of human trust—a play where actors, often unseen and disguised, manipulate emotions and perceptions to achieve their objectives. In this section, we'll unravel the human-centric dimensions of various types of social engineering attacks, understanding their nuances, motivations, and impact, all while avoiding technical jargon.

Phishing: The Crafty Deception

Phishing is the chameleon of social engineering attacks, adapting its guise to match the surroundings. It involves the creation of deceptive emails, messages, or websites that appear legitimate, often mimicking trusted entities such as banks, social media platforms, or government agencies. The aim is to lure individuals into providing sensitive information, such as passwords or credit card details, by exploiting trust in familiar communication channels.

Pretexting: Crafting Convincing Narratives

Pretexting is the art of storytelling in the world of social engineering. Attackers create elaborate scenarios or pretexts to trick individuals into divulging information or performing actions that compromise security. This may involve posing as a coworker, service provider, or authority figure, weaving a convincing narrative to gain the trust of the target. The success of pretexting hinges on the human tendency to trust and be cooperative.

Impersonation: The Masquerade of Trust

Impersonation is the masked ball of social engineering, where attackers don the guise of someone familiar or authoritative. This can take the form of impersonating a colleague, IT personnel, or even a company executive. By exploiting trust in known figures, attackers seek to gain access to secure areas, sensitive information, or convince individuals to perform actions they wouldn't under normal circumstances.

Baiting: The Tempting Offer

Baiting is the lure strategically placed in the path of human curiosity. Attackers may leave infected USB drives or enticing links in public spaces, counting on individuals' innate curiosity to take the bait. Once the bait is taken, it can lead to the compromise of systems or the introduction of malware. Baiting exploits the temptation for something seemingly valuable or intriguing.

Quizzes and Surveys: Unveiling Personal Details

Quizzes and surveys become the Trojan horses of social engineering, seemingly harmless on the surface but concealing hidden dangers. Individuals are enticed to participate in quizzes that ask seemingly innocuous questions, often collecting personal information along the way. This information can then be exploited for identity theft, unauthorized access, or other malicious purposes.

Spear Phishing: Precision in Deception

Spear phishing is the sniper rifle of social engineering, targeting specific individuals with tailored and highly personalized attacks. Unlike generic phishing attempts, spear phishing involves detailed reconnaissance on the target, using information such as job roles, relationships, or recent activities to craft convincing and targeted messages. The precision makes spear phishing highly effective in breaching defenses.

Vising: Voice-Based Deception

Vising, or voice phishing, brings social engineering into the realm of phone calls. Attackers use phone calls to impersonate trusted entities, such as bank representatives or IT support. Through persuasive communication, they aim to extract sensitive information or convince individuals to take actions that compromise security. Vising exploits the trust placed in auditory communication.

Watering Hole Attacks: Ambushing Digital Hangouts

Watering hole attacks mirror the strategic patience of a predator waiting at a watering hole for its prey. Attackers identify websites frequented by their targets and compromise these sites with malware. When individuals visit these trusted digital hangouts, they unknowingly expose themselves to malicious code, leading to potential security breaches.

The Impact on Human Trust: A Symphony of Deception

Beyond the technicalities, the true essence of social engineering attacks lies in the impact they have on human trust—the fragile thread that binds our digital interactions. Picture this impact as a symphony of deception—each type of attack playing a distinct note in the orchestrated manipulation:

Erosion of Digital Trust

Social engineering attacks erode the digital trust individuals place in online interactions. Just as a drop of ink diffuses in water, these attacks spread uncertainty and skepticism, making individuals more cautious in their online engagements.

Financial Consequences

Consider the financial consequences as the toll of a persuasive performance. Social engineering attacks can lead to significant financial losses, whether through unauthorized access to bank accounts, fraudulent transactions, or identity theft. The impact resonates not only in the digital realm but also in tangible financial repercussions.

Privacy Breaches

Imagine privacy breaches as the unwanted spotlight on personal lives. Successful social engineering attacks often result in the compromise of sensitive personal information, exposing individuals to the risk of identity theft, stalking, or other forms of malicious exploitation.

Organizational Vulnerability

Think of organizational vulnerability as the Achilles' heel of businesses and institutions. Social engineering attacks targeting employees can lead to unauthorized access to corporate networks, exposure of sensitive company information, and potential reputational damage. The consequences extend beyond individuals to impact the interconnected web of business relationships and operations.

HOW TO PREVENT SOCIAL ENGINEERING ATTACKS

In the intricate landscape of digital interactions, safeguarding against social engineering attacks becomes a nuanced dance between awareness, skepticism, and proactive measures. Imagine it as the art of fortifying the castle against subtle infiltrators—knowing the faces of friends from those of foes and fortifying the walls against manipulation. In this exploration, we'll unravel the human-centric dimensions of preventing social engineering attacks, offering practical insights and strategies that resonate with our everyday experiences, all while avoiding technical jargon.

Cultivate Digital Literacy: Nurturing a Skeptical Mindset

In the realm of social engineering, the first line of defense is a well-cultivated sense of digital literacy. Just as we navigate the nuances of language, understanding the digital landscape empowers individuals to discern between authentic communication and deceptive tactics. This involves recognizing red flags in emails, messages, or websites, questioning unsolicited requests for information, and staying informed about prevalent social engineering techniques.

Stay Informed About Common Tactics: Recognizing the Deceptive Playbook

Imagine staying informed about common social engineering tactics as studying the moves of a chess opponent. By understanding the deceptive playbook, individuals can better recognize when they are being targeted. Familiarizing oneself with phishing techniques, pretexting scenarios, and the various types of social engineering attacks provides a crucial layer of defense against manipulation.

Verify the Source: Trust, but Verify

Trust lies at the heart of social engineering attacks, and one effective defense is to adopt the mantra "trust, but verify." Just as we confirm the identity of someone at our doorstep, verifying the legitimacy of digital communications is essential. This involves double-checking email addresses, contacting organizations directly through trusted channels to confirm requests, and using official websites for sensitive transactions.

Implement Two-Factor Authentication: Adding an Extra Layer of Security

Two-factor authentication (2FA) acts as the digital equivalent of a second lock on the door. By requiring an additional step, such as a code sent to a mobile device, 2FA adds an extra layer of security, making it more challenging for attackers to gain unauthorized access. Enabling 2FA on various online accounts significantly reduces the risk of falling victim to social engineering attacks.

Be Wary of Unsolicited Communication: The Stranger Danger Principle

Imagine unsolicited communication in the digital realm as akin to a stranger knocking on your door. Being wary of unexpected emails, messages, or calls is crucial. Social engineers often rely on unsolicited communication to initiate their deceptive tactics. By approaching unexpected interactions with skepticism and caution, individuals can mitigate the risk of falling prey to manipulative tactics.

Educate Employees and Team Members: Creating a Collective Defense

In organizational settings, educating employees becomes a collective defense strategy. Just as a well-informed army is more resilient against infiltration, a workforce aware of social engineering risks is better equipped to recognize and report potential threats. Conducting regular training sessions, sharing real-world examples, and fostering a culture of cybersecurity awareness contribute to a robust defense against social engineering attacks.

Use Secure Communication Channels: Building Fortified Pathways

Secure communication channels act as the fortified pathways that protect sensitive information. Just as we choose secure routes for valuable cargo, using encrypted communication tools, secure websites (https ://), and trusted messaging platforms ensures that information travels through protected channels. This adds a layer of defense against interception and manipulation by social engineers.

Keep Software and Systems Updated: Sealing Potential Entry Points

Imagine software updates as reinforcing the castle walls against potential breaches. Regularly updating software and systems is essential for closing security vulnerabilities that attackers may exploit. By staying current with security patches, individuals and organizations minimize the risk of falling victim to social engineering attacks that target outdated or unpatched software.

Foster a Culture of Open Communication: Breaking the Silence Barrier

In both personal and professional settings, fostering a culture of open communication acts as a silent alarm against social engineering threats. Just as trust is built on transparent dialogue, encouraging individuals to report suspicious incidents without fear of reprisal creates a collective defense mechanism. This ensures that potential threats are addressed promptly and effectively.

Conduct Security Audits: Periodic Checking of Defenses

Security audits serve as the periodic checking of defenses—a thorough examination to identify and address vulnerabilities. Organizations can conduct regular security audits to assess the effectiveness of their security measures, identify potential weak points, and implement corrective actions. This proactive approach ensures that defenses remain resilient against evolving social engineering tactics.

Chapter 8

CRYPTOGRAPHY AND ENCRYPTION

OVERVIEW OF CRYPTOGRAPHY AND ENCRYPTION

In the realm of digital communication, where information flows like a vast river, cryptography and encryption emerge as the silent guardians, ensuring the confidentiality and integrity of our sensitive data. Picture them as the locks and keys in the digital world—a means of securing messages and transactions in an era where information is the currency of communication. In this exploration, let's unravel the human-centric dimensions of cryptography and encryption, understanding the basics without delving into technical intricacies.

The Art of Secret Writing: Overview of Cryptography

Cryptography, often referred to as the art of secret writing, has been a part of human history for centuries. Imagine it as the ancient practice of sealing messages with wax or encoding them with symbols—a way to convey information securely. In the digital era, cryptography has evolved into a sophisticated science, serving as the backbone of secure communication and online transactions.

Confidentiality at its Core

At the heart of cryptography lies the concept of confidentiality. In the digital context, this means ensuring that only authorized parties can understand the contents of a message. Whether it's a private conversation, a financial transaction, or sensitive corporate data, cryptography acts as the digital envelope, shielding information from prying eyes.

Encrypting and Decrypting Secrets

Cryptography involves two key players—the sender and the recipient. The sender uses an encryption algorithm and a secret key to convert plain text into an unreadable format known as cipher text. On the other end, the recipient, armed with a corresponding decryption key, transforms the cipher text back into its original form. This process creates a secure channel through which information can be shared without fear of interception.

Symmetric vs. Asymmetric Cryptography

Imagine symmetric cryptography as a shared secret between two friends. In this scenario, both the sender and recipient use the same key for encryption and decryption. It's like having a secret language that only the two friends understand. On the flip side, asymmetric cryptography introduces a pair of keys—one for encryption and one for decryption. It's like having a public mailbox where anyone can drop a letter (encrypted with the public key), but only the owner of the mailbox can unlock and read it (using the private key).

The Digital Envelope: Understanding Encryption

Encryption, the practical manifestation of cryptography, serves as the digital envelope that wraps messages in a protective layer. Think of it as the lock on your front door—a mechanism that ensures only those with the correct key can access what's inside.

Securing Data in Transit

Just as you would seal a physical letter in an envelope before sending it, encryption secures data as it travels across digital channels. When you make an online purchase, log in to your email, or send a message through a messaging app, encryption shields the information from being intercepted by malicious actors.

Protecting Stored Information

Consider encryption as the guardian of your digital diary. When information is stored on devices or servers, encryption ensures that even if someone gains unauthorized access, the data remains unreadable without the proper decryption key. This adds an extra layer of defense in the event of theft or data breaches.

Authentication and Integrity

Encryption not only conceals the content of messages but also plays a role in authentication and integrity. Imagine a digital signature as a seal of authenticity on a letter. By encrypting a hash (a unique identifier) of the message with a private key, the sender can prove both the origin of the message and its integrity—ensuring it hasn't been altered during transmission.

Everyday Encounters: Where Encryption Works Behind the Scenes

In our digital lives, encryption quietly works behind the scenes, securing our interactions in ways we might not always be aware of.

Secure Browsing (HTTPS)

When you visit a website with "https://" in the URL, he's' stands for secure, indicating that the communication between your browser and the website is encrypted. This is crucial for protecting sensitive information like login credentials and payment details.

End-to-End Messaging Encryption

Messaging apps often employ end-to-end encryption, ensuring that only the intended recipients can read the messages. Even if the messages pass through servers, they remain encrypted and indecipherable without the proper keys.

Encrypted Email Communication

Some email services offer encryption options, allowing users to send and receive encrypted emails. This ensures that the contents of the email are accessible only to the intended recipient.

Challenges and Considerations in the Cryptographic Landscape

While cryptography and encryption provide a robust framework for securing digital communication, it's essential to recognize the challenges and considerations in this ever- evolving landscape.

Key Management

Managing encryption keys is a critical aspect of cryptographic systems. Whether it's ensuring the secure distribution of keys or handling key rotations, effective key management is vital for maintaining the security of encrypted communications.

Balancing Security and Usability

Striking the right balance between security and usability is an ongoing challenge. Complex encryption processes that hinder user experience may discourage adoption, emphasizing the need for solutions that seamlessly integrate strong encryption without sacrificing user- friendliness.

Adaptability to Emerging Threats

Cryptographic algorithms need to evolve to withstand emerging threats. The landscape of cyber threats is dynamic, and as computing power increases, encryption methods must adapt to maintain their effectiveness.

COMMON ENCRYPTION METHODS AND ALGORITHMS

In the intricate world of digital communication, where the exchange of information is a constant dance, encryption methods and algorithms serve as the guardians of confidentiality and security. Picture them as the diverse array of locks and keys in a vast digital kingdom—a means of securing messages and transactions in an age where data is both the currency and the commodity. In this exploration, let's unravel the human-centric dimensions of common encryption methods and algorithms, understanding the basics without diving into technical complexities.

Symmetric Encryption: Sharing a Secret Language

Imagine symmetric encryption as sharing a secret language between two parties—a language only they understand. In this scenario, both the sender and recipient use the same secret key to encrypt and decrypt messages. It's akin to having a shared key to a locked box: if you have the key, you can lock and unlock it. Popular symmetric encryption algorithms include Advanced Encryption Standard (AES) and Data Encryption Standard (DES).

AES (Advanced Encryption Standard)

Think of AES as the maestro orchestrating a symphony of security. Widely adopted for its efficiency and strength, AES operates on blocks of data and supports key sizes of 128, 192, or 256 bits. Like a well-protected vault, AES ensures that even if someone intercepts the data, they can't decipher it without the proper key.

DES (Data Encryption Standard)

Consider DES as the elder statesman of symmetric encryption. While less commonly used today due to its 56-bit key size vulnerability, DES played a pivotal role in the history of cryptography. It encrypts data in 64-bit blocks, and despite its age, understanding DES provides insights into the evolution of encryption.

Asymmetric Encryption: Two Keys, One Pair

Asymmetric encryption introduces a duo of keys—a pair that works in tandem but with distinct roles. Imagine it as having two keys to your home: one opens the door, and the other locks it. The keys are mathematically related, but you can't deduce one from the other.

RSA (Rivets–Shamir–Adleman)

Think of RSA as the mathematician's masterpiece. Named after its creators, RSA is widely used for securing communications on the internet. It involves a pair of keys—a public key for encryption and a private key for decryption. Messages encrypted with the public key can only be decrypted with the corresponding private key, ensuring secure communication between parties.

ECC (Elliptic Curve Cryptography)

Consider ECC as the efficient minimalist in asymmetric cryptography. It leverages the mathematics of elliptic curves to create smaller key sizes while maintaining robust security. ECC is particularly valuable in resource- constrained environments, making it a popular choice for mobile devices and Internet of Things (IoT) devices.

Hash Functions: The Digital Fingerprint

Hash functions play a crucial role in ensuring data integrity and authentication. Imagine a hash function as the digital fingerprint of a file—a unique identifier created through a one-way mathematical process. Even a slight change in the file results in a vastly different hash.

SHA-256 (Secure Hash Algorithm 256-bit)

Think of SHA-256 as the sculptor creating intricate fingerprints. Part of the SHA-2 family, SHA-256 produces a fixed-size 256-bit hash value. It's widely used in block chain technology, digital signatures, and certificate authorities to verify the integrity of data.

MD5 (Message Digest Algorithm 5)

Consider MD5 as the veteran of hash functions. While once widely used, MD5 is now considered insecure for cryptographic purposes due to vulnerabilities that allow attackers to generate collisions—different inputs producing the same hash. However, MD5 is still used in non-security contexts, such as checksums for file integrity.

Hybrid Cryptography: Blending Strengths

In the vast encryption landscape, hybrid cryptography emerges as a harmonious blend of symmetric and asymmetric approaches. Picture it as a dual-key system: asymmetric encryption is used to securely exchange a shared secret key, which is then employed for the actual encryption and decryption using symmetric techniques.

TLS/SSL Protocols

Think of TLS (Transport Layer Security) and its predecessor SSL (Secure Sockets Layer) as the sentinels safeguarding your online transactions. These protocols employ a hybrid approach, using asymmetric encryption to exchange symmetric keys for securing the data exchanged between web browsers and servers. They create a secure and encrypted connection, ensuring the confidentiality and integrity of the transmitted information.

Quantum-Safe Cryptography: Preparing for Tomorrow's Challenges

As technology advances, the quantum era looms on the horizon, presenting challenges to traditional cryptographic methods. Quantum-safe cryptography is the knight in shining armor preparing for this future. It involves algorithms that resist attacks from quantum computers, which could potentially break currently secure encryption methods.

Post-Quantum Cryptography

Consider post-quantum cryptography as the forward- thinking strategist. It explores algorithms that, even in the face of quantum computing power, maintain their resilience. Candidates include lattice-based cryptography, hash-based cryptography, and code-based cryptography, each designed to withstand quantum attacks.

Considerations in Choosing Encryption Methods: Balancing Act

In selecting encryption methods, a balancing act between security, efficiency, and practicality comes into play. Different scenarios call for different approaches, and understanding these considerations is vital.

Key Length

Think of key length as the strength of a lock. Longer keys generally provide greater security, but they also require more computational resources. The balance between key length and computational efficiency is a critical consideration.

Computational Resources

Consider computational resources as the horsepower of a system. Some encryption methods, especially those with longer key lengths, demand more processing power. In resource-constrained environments, efficiency becomes a crucial factor in selecting appropriate encryption methods.

Use Case and Context

In the encryption landscape, there's no one-size-fits-all solution. The choice of encryption methods depends on the specific use case and the context in which they are deployed. What works well for securing internet communications may not be the best fit for encrypting sensitive data on a resource- constrained IoT device.

PUBLIC KEY INFRASTRUCTURE (PKI)

In the vast landscape of digital communication, where security is paramount, Public Key Infrastructure (PKI) emerges as a crucial framework—a sophisticated system of digital IDs, keys, and certificates that orchestrates the secure exchange of information in the digital realm. Imagine PKI as the invisible but robust guardian ensuring the confidentiality, integrity, and authenticity of our online interactions. In this exploration, let's unravel the human-centric dimensions of PKI, understanding the basics without delving into technical intricacies.

The Foundation: Keys and Certificates

At the heart of PKI lie cryptographic keys—a pair of keys, to be precise. Imagine these keys as a digital lock and key duo, where one key (the public key) is shared openly, and its counterpart (the private key) is kept secret. This pair enables a secure communication dance, where information encrypted with the public key can only be decrypted with the corresponding private key.

Public Key

Think of the public key as an open invitation. It's shared openly and can be freely distributed to anyone. Like a mailbox with an open slot, the public key allows others to encrypt messages or verify signatures.

Private Key

Consider the private key as the closely guarded secret. It's known only to the key owner and is used for decrypting messages or creating digital signatures. The private key is akin to the key that unlocks the mailbox—it must be kept secure to maintain the integrity of the communication.

Certificates act as the digital IDs in this cryptographic ballet. Imagine a certificate as a notarized document verifying the identity of the key owner. It includes the public key and information about the key owner, all signed by a trusted third party called a Certificate Authority (CA). This CA serves as the digital notary, vouching for the legitimacy of the public key and the identity associated with it.

The Players: Certificate Authority, End Users, and Registration Authority

Certificate Authority (CA)

Picture the CA as the trusted referee in a game. It verifies the identity of individuals or entities requesting digital certificates. Once verified, the CA issues the digital certificate, essentially endorsing the legitimacy of the public key and its owner. Popular CAs include companies like DigiCert, Let's Encrypt, and Sectigo.

End Users

Envision end users as the participants in the secure communication dance. They generate key pairs, obtain digital certificates, and use them to encrypt messages, verify signatures, or establish secure connections.

Registration Authority (RA)

Think of the RA as the assistant to the referee. In some PKI setups, an RA assists the CA by validating the identity of certificate requesters. It acts as a bridge between end users and the CA, streamlining the verification process.

Applications of PKI: Enabling Secure Transactions

Secure Web Browsing (HTTPS)

Consider secure web browsing as a grand ball where PKI orchestrates the dance of secure connections. When you visit a website with "https://" in the URL, PKI is at play. Your browser checks the website's digital certificate, ensuring it's valid and issued by a trusted CA. This secure connection encrypts data exchanged between your browser and the website, safeguarding your sensitive information.

Email Encryption and Digital Signatures

Imagine email communication as a sealed letter protected by PKI. By using digital signatures, senders can verify the authenticity of their messages, ensuring they haven't been tampered with. Encryption, facilitated by PKI, ensures that only the intended recipient can decrypt and read the contents.

Virtual Private Networks (VPNs)

Picture a VPN as a private tunnel in the digital landscape, and PKI as the architect ensuring its security. PKI enables the establishment of secure VPN connections, encrypting data transmitted between your device and the VPN server. This safeguards your online activities, particularly important when accessing public Wi-Fi networks.

Challenges and Considerations in the PKI Landscape:

While PKI is a powerful tool in securing digital communication, it comes with its own set of challenges and considerations.

Certificate Lifecycle Management

Think of certificate lifecycle management as the choreography of a ballet. Certificates have a lifespan, and managing their issuance, renewal, and revocation requires careful coordination. Ensuring that certificates are valid and up-to-date is crucial for maintaining a secure PKI ecosystem.

Key Management

Consider key management as the backstage security team. Safeguarding private keys is paramount, as compromise can lead to severe security breaches. PKI systems must implement robust key management practices to protect against unauthorized access.

Trust Hierarchy

Picture the trust hierarchy in PKI as the tiered seating arrangement in a theater. Trust relies on the hierarchy of CAs. While some CAs are widely trusted (root CAs), others derive trust from being linked to these root authorities. Maintaining a secure and trustworthy hierarchy is essential for the integrity of PKI.

UNDERSTANDING DIGITAL SIGNATURES AND CERTIFICATES

In the expansive world of digital communication, where trust and security are paramount, digital signatures and certificates emerge as the guardians of authenticity and integrity. Picture them as the digital equivalents of a handwritten signature and an official seal—a means of verifying the identity of senders and ensuring the unaltered state of messages in the vast landscape of online interactions. In this exploration, let's unravel the human-centric dimensions of digital signatures and certificates, understanding the basics without diving into technical complexities.

The Essence of Digital Signatures: A Virtual Handshake

Imagine sending a digital document as a sealed letter. In the physical world, you might sign the letter to authenticate it. In the digital realm, a digital signature serves this purpose. Think of a digital signature as a virtual handshake—a way for the sender to say, "This is really from me, and the content hasn't been tampered with."

Private Key

Picture the private key as your unique, closely guarded signature. Just as you sign a physical document with your unique handwriting, the private key is used to create the digital signature. It's known only to you, adding a layer of exclusivity and security.

Public Key

Consider the public key as the counterpart to your signature. It's freely shared, allowing anyone to verify the authenticity of the digital signature. Like checking the signature against a known handwriting sample, the public key is used to verify that the digital signature matches the sender's private key.

Hash Function:

Think of the hash function as the digital fingerprint of the document. Before signing, the document's content is processed through a one-way mathematical function, creating a fixed-size string of characters—a unique identifier for that specific content.

Creating the Digital Signature

Envision creating a digital signature as the act of signing the sealed letter. The private key is applied to the hash of the document, generating the digital signature. This signature, like a seal on an envelope, ensures the document's authenticity and integrity.

Verifying Digital Signatures: A Trustworthy Unveiling

Imagine receiving a sealed letter with a signature. Before opening, you want to ensure it's from the claimed sender and hasn't been tampered with. Verifying a digital signature follows a similar process:

Public Key of the Sender

Picture the public key as the known signature sample. Just as you'd use a known signature to verify authenticity, the recipient uses the sender's public key to verify the digital signature.

Hash Function

Think of the hash function as the trusted notary. The recipient applies the same hash function to the received document, creating a new digital fingerprint.

Verification

Envision verifying the digital signature as the act of comparing signatures. Using the public key, the recipient checks if the generated digital signature matches the one received. If the signatures match, it's a trustworthy indication that the document is authentic and hasn't been altered.

Certificates: The Trusted Notary Public

Certificates serve as the digital notary public in this virtual world. Imagine a certificate as a notarized document vouching for the authenticity of your signature. It includes:

Public Key

Picture the public key in the certificate as your endorsed signature. It's accompanied by information about you or your organization, creating a digital ID.

Digital Signature of the Certificate Authority (CA)

Consider the CA's digital signature as the notary's official seal. The CA, a trusted third party, signs the certificate, endorsing the legitimacy of the public key and the associated identity.

Expiration Date

Think of the expiration date as the notary's term of validity. Certificates have a lifespan, and their legitimacy is valid until the expiration date.

Applications in Everyday Digital Life: Securing Transactions

Secure Email Communication

Imagine sending sensitive information via email as a sealed envelope. By digitally signing your email, you provide recipients with a way to verify its authenticity, ensuring they receive legitimate communication.

Code Signing

Picture code signing as the official stamp on software. Developers sign their code with a digital signature, allowing users to verify that the software hasn't been tampered with and comes from the claimed source.

Document Authentication

Envision document authentication as the notarization of digital documents. By digitally signing a document, you assure recipients of its origin and integrity, akin to notarizing a physical document.

Challenges and Considerations in Digital Signatures and Certificates

While digital signatures and certificates enhance online security, they come with their own set of challenges and considerations:

Key Management

Consider key management as the responsibility of safeguarding your signature. Protecting private keys is crucial, as compromise could lead to unauthorized access or forged digital signatures.

Certificate Authority Trust

Picture the trust in CAs as the foundation of the notary system. Trust relies on the credibility of CAs. Users need to trust that the CA has verified the identity of the certificate holder accurately.

Certificate Revocation

Think of certificate revocation as the recall of a notary's stamp. If a private key is compromised or if the certificate needs to be invalidated for any reason, a mechanism for revocation is essential.

Chapter 9

RISK MANAGEMENT, INCIDENT RESPONSE AND DISASTER RECOVERY

IDENTIFYING AND ASSESSING RISK

In the intricate landscape of cybersecurity, where the digital realm meets the ever-evolving threat landscape, risk management emerges as the sentinel standing guard against potential hazards. Think of it as a vigilant gatekeeper, assessing the vulnerabilities and potential impacts that could compromise the security of an organization's digital assets. In this exploration, we delve into the human-centric dimensions of identifying and assessing risks, navigating the delicate balance between innovation and security.

The Foundations of Risk Management: A Digital Chessboard

Imagine the digital landscape as a vast chessboard where every move carries inherent risks. Risk management is the strategist carefully analyzing each piece, predicting potential threats, and fortifying the defenses.

Risk Identification

Picture risk identification as the act of scouting the chessboard. It involves identifying and cataloging potential threats and vulnerabilities that could impact the organization's objectives. These could range from external cyber threats to internal weaknesses in processes or systems.

Asset Valuation

Consider asset valuation as assigning value to each chess piece. In the digital realm, assets include not only tangible elements like servers and databases but also intangible assets such as intellectual property and customer data. Assigning value helps prioritize the protection of critical assets.

Threat Assessment

Think of threat assessment as evaluating the opponent's moves. Understanding the nature and capabilities of potential threats is crucial. This involves considering external threats like hackers and malware, as well as internal threats such as employee negligence or system failures.

Vulnerability Analysis

Envision vulnerability analysis as examining the weaknesses in your defenses. Just as a chess player looks for weak points in the opponent's position, vulnerability analysis involves identifying potential weaknesses in systems, processes, or policies that could be exploited by attackers.

Balancing Act: Innovation vs. Security

In the dynamic digital realm, organizations constantly strive for innovation while simultaneously guarding against potential risks. It's a delicate balancing act where risk management plays a pivotal role.

Innovation as a Catalyst

Picture innovation as the catalyst propelling pieces across the chessboard. Organizations embrace new technologies, processes, and business models to stay competitive. However, each innovation introduces new elements that may carry inherent risks.

Risk Appetite and Tolerance

Consider risk appetite and tolerance as the strategic stance on the chessboard. Risk appetite defines how much risk an organization is willing to accept to achieve its objectives, while risk tolerance establishes the acceptable level of variation in achieving those objectives. This balance ensures that the pursuit of innovation doesn't compromise the overall security posture.

Continuous Monitoring

Think of continuous monitoring as the watchful eye on the chessboard. In the digital landscape, risks evolve, and new threats emerge. Continuous monitoring ensures that organizations stay abreast of changes in the threat landscape and can adapt their risk management strategies accordingly.

Real-world Application: A Digital Chess Match

Picture an e-commerce platform as a player in this digital chess match. It aims to innovate by introducing a new payment processing system to enhance user experience. However, this innovation introduces potential risks:

Risk Identification

The organization identifies potential risks, including the possibility of payment data breaches, system vulnerabilities, and increased exposure to cyber threats.

Asset Valuation

The e-commerce platform values critical assets, such as customer payment data and the reputation of the brand, assigning them high priority for protection.

Threat Assessment

The organization assesses potential threats, considering the likelihood of cyber-attacks, data breaches, and the capabilities of adversaries seeking to exploit the new payment system.

Vulnerability Analysis

A thorough analysis reveals potential vulnerabilities in the new payment processing system, such as weak encryption protocols or insufficient security measures.

Incident Response: Navigating the Unexpected Chess Move

In the dynamic digital chess match, incident response serves as the player's strategy for navigating unexpected moves and mitigating the impact of security incidents.

Incident Identification

Imagine incident identification as recognizing the unexpected chess move. Incidents could range from a data breach to a system outage. Incident response involves swiftly identifying and acknowledging that an adverse event has occurred.

Containment and Eradication

Consider containment and eradication as the strategic response to the unexpected move. In chess, it might involve sacrificing a pawn to gain positional advantage. In incident response, it entails isolating and neutralizing the threat to prevent further damage.

Communication and Coordination

Picture communication and coordination as the collaborative efforts of players on the chessboard. In the digital realm, effective communication ensures that stakeholders are informed, and coordinated efforts are undertaken to address the incident.

Learning from the Move

Envision learning from the move as the post-incident analysis. Just as chess players review games to learn from their mistakes, incident response involves analyzing the incident to understand its root cause, identify improvements, and enhance future resilience.

Disaster Recovery: Rebuilding After a Checkmate Move

In the unfortunate event of a checkmate move—where the impact of an incident is severe—disaster recovery comes into play. Think of it as the player's strategy for rebuilding and restoring normalcy.

Recovery Planning

Picture recovery planning as the strategy for rebuilding after a checkmate move. Organizations develop plans that outline the steps and processes to restore critical systems and services.

Backup and Restoration

Consider backup and restoration as the regaining of lost pieces on the chessboard. Regularly backing up critical data and systems ensures that, in the event of a disaster, organizations can restore operations to a known and functional state.

Infrastructure Resilience

Think of infrastructure resilience as fortifying the chess pieces. In the digital realm, this involves designing systems and networks to be resilient, capable of withstanding and recovering from disruptions.

Training and Drills

Envision training and drills as the practice matches before the actual game. Organizations conduct regular drills to test the effectiveness of their disaster recovery plans, ensuring that teams are well-prepared to respond in a real- world scenario.

RISK MITIGATION STRATEGIES

In the dynamic landscape of business and technology, where opportunities and challenges coexist, the art of risk mitigation emerges as a crucial skill—a strategic approach to minimize the impact of potential setbacks. Imagine it as the seasoned navigator steering a ship through unpredictable waters, anticipating storms, and ensuring a safe journey. In this exploration, we unravel the human-centric dimensions of risk mitigation strategies, navigating the delicate balance between ambition and prudence.

Understanding Risk Mitigation: A Journey of Preparedness

Picture an organization as a ship embarking on a journey. While the voyage promises new horizons and opportunities, it also exposes the ship to potential storms and unforeseen challenges. Risk mitigation is the captain's approach to prepare for and navigate through these challenges effectively.

Identifying Potential Storms

Consider risk identification as the first mate's duty of scanning the horizon for potential storms. This involves a comprehensive assessment to identify and catalog potential risks—ranging from market volatility and technological disruptions to regulatory changes and cybersecurity threats.

Assessing the Sea Worthiness

Imagine risk assessment as the shipwright evaluating the sea-worthiness of the vessel. It involves evaluating the potential impact and likelihood of each identified risk. Some risks may pose immediate threats, while others may be on the distant horizon.

Charting the Course

Think of risk mitigation planning as the navigator charting the course. Based on the identified risks, organizations develop a strategic plan that outlines how to navigate through potential challenges. This plan considers both preventive measures and responsive actions.

Strategies for the Journey: Navigating Through Risk

In the vast sea of potential risks, organizations employ a range of strategies to navigate safely. These strategies are the sails and rudders that enable the ship to adjust its course and weather the storms.

Diversification as a Sturdy Hull

Picture diversification as reinforcing the ship's hull. Just as a sturdy hull withstands rough seas, a diversified portfolio of products, services, or markets can help organizations weather economic downturns or shifts in consumer preferences.

Insurance as a Lifeboat

Consider insurance as the lifeboat on standby. While the ship aims to avoid storms, having insurance in place provides a safety net. It helps mitigate financial losses in the event of unforeseen incidents, such as natural disasters or accidents.

Cybersecurity Measures as the Ship's Defense System

Think of cybersecurity measures as the defense system against digital threats. In today's interconnected world, cyber attacks pose significant risks. Implementing robust cybersecurity measures, such as firewalls, encryption, and regular security audits, helps protect the organization's digital assets.

Contingency Planning as the Emergency Protocol

Envision contingency planning as the emergency protocol. Just as ships have emergency procedures, organizations develop contingency plans that outline steps to be taken in the face of unexpected events. This could involve having backup systems, alternative suppliers, or crisis communication plans.

Balancing Act: Innovation and Risk

In the quest for innovation, organizations constantly navigate the balance between pushing boundaries and managing risks. It's akin to deciding when to set sail for uncharted waters and when to anchor in a safe harbor.

Innovation as Uncharted Waters

Picture innovation as the decision to set sail for uncharted waters. New technologies, business models, or market expansions carry inherent risks. Organizations embrace innovation but do so with a keen awareness of potential challenges.

Risk Monitoring as the Navigator's Compass

Consider risk monitoring as the navigator's compass. In the journey of innovation, continuous monitoring of the risk landscape is essential. This involves staying attuned to market trends, regulatory changes, and emerging technologies that could impact the organization's course.

Adaptive Strategies as Course Adjustments

Think of adaptive strategies as the ability to adjust the ship's course in real-time. In a dynamic environment, organizations must be agile. Adaptive strategies allow for quick adjustments based on changing circumstances, ensuring that the ship stays on a safe and prosperous course.

Real-world Application: A Seafaring Company's Odyssey

Imagine a seafaring company aiming to expand its routes to new, potentially lucrative territories. This expansion, while promising, comes with inherent risks:

Risk Identification

The company identifies potential risks, including economic instability in the new markets, geopolitical uncertainties, and challenges in adapting to local regulations and cultural nuances.

Assessment of Sea Worthiness

The company assesses the potential impact of each risk, recognizing that economic downturns could impact profitability, geopolitical tensions might disrupt operations, and cultural missteps could harm the brand's reputation.

Charting the Course with Mitigation Strategies

Armed with this understanding, the company develops a risk mitigation plan. Diversification is employed by expanding gradually into the new markets rather than making a massive leap. Insurance is secured to mitigate financial losses in case of unexpected challenges, and contingency plans are established to address unforeseen circumstances.

Human Elements of Risk Mitigation: A Crew's Role

In the maritime world, the crew's competence, communication, and adaptability are essential for a safe journey. Similarly, the human elements play a crucial role in the success of risk mitigation strategies.

Employee Training and Competence

Consider employee training as the crew's preparation for the journey. Well-trained and competent employees are better equipped to identify and respond to potential risks. Training programs ensure that the crew understands the organization's risk mitigation strategies.

Communication and Collaboration

Think of communication as the ship's radio connecting the crew. Effective communication within the organization fosters a culture of risk awareness. Employees at all levels should feel empowered to communicate potential risks and contribute to the ongoing improvement of risk mitigation measures.

Adaptability and Resilience

Envision adaptability as the crew's ability to adjust sails in changing winds. Organizations must cultivate adaptability and resilience. When unforeseen challenges arise, a flexible and resilient workforce can navigate through adversity and contribute to effective risk mitigation.

CREATING A RISK MANAGEMENT PLAN

In the unpredictable landscape of business and technology, where opportunities and challenges intersect, the creation of a risk management plan becomes the compass guiding an organization through uncharted waters. Imagine this plan as a meticulously crafted map, charting the course through potential storms and unforeseen challenges. In this exploration, we unravel the human-centric dimensions of creating a risk management plan, navigating the delicate balance between ambition and prudence.

Setting the Stage: Acknowledging the Business Landscape

Picture an organization as a vessel setting sail on a grand expedition. While the journey promises new territories and opportunities, it also exposes the ship to potential storms and unforeseen challenges. Creating a risk management plan is akin to the captain's strategic approach, preparing the crew and the ship for the unpredictable voyage ahead.

Understanding the Terrain

Consider understanding the terrain as the first mate's responsibility. This involves a thorough assessment of the business landscape—identifying potential risks that could impact the organization's objectives. These risks could range from market volatility and technological disruptions to regulatory changes and cybersecurity threats.

Mapping the Assets

Imagine mapping the assets as the cartographer's task. Assets, both tangible and intangible, are critical components of the journey. These could include financial resources, human capital, intellectual property, and the organization's reputation. Assigning value to each asset helps prioritize their protection.

Assessing Potential Threats

Think of assessing potential threats as the meteorologist predicting the weather. Understanding the potential threats involves evaluating the nature and capabilities of adversaries or challenges. This could include external threats like cyberattacks, natural disasters, or economic downturns, as well as internal threats like operational failures or human errors.

Crafting the Plan: Navigating Through Uncertainty

In the face of potential challenges, a well-crafted risk management plan serves as the navigator's guide, ensuring that the ship is equipped to navigate through uncertainty effectively.

Risk Identification and Categorization

Picture risk identification and categorization as plotting the known routes on the map. This involves systematically identifying and cataloging potential risks. Risks can be categorized based on their nature—strategic, operational, financial, or compliance-related. Each category requires tailored strategies for mitigation.

Risk Assessment and Prioritization

Consider risk assessment and prioritization as determining the importance of various routes. Organizations assess the potential impact and likelihood of each identified risk. Prioritizing risks helps focus resources on addressing the most critical threats that could significantly impact the achievement of business objectives.

Mitigation Strategies

Think of mitigation strategies as the arsenal of tools to navigate through potential challenges. Depending on the nature of the risks, organizations deploy various strategies. These could include risk avoidance (altering business practices to avoid certain risks), risk reduction (implementing measures to minimize the impact of risks), risk transfer (outsourcing or obtaining insurance), or risk acceptance (acknowledging and budgeting for certain risks).

Monitoring and Review

Envision monitoring and review as the ongoing navigation of the journey. The risk management plan is not static; it requires continuous monitoring and periodic reviews. This ensures that the plan remains aligned with the evolving business landscape and can be adjusted in response to new risks or changes in existing ones.

Navigating Human Elements: Engaging the Crew

In the maritime world, the crew's competence, communication, and adaptability are essential for a safe journey. Similarly, the human elements play a crucial role in the success of a risk management plan.

Employee Training and Awareness

Consider employee training as preparing the crew for the journey. Well-trained and aware employees are better equipped to identify and respond to potential risks. Training programs ensure that the entire team understands the organization's risk management strategies.

Communication and Collaboration

Think of communication as the ship's radio connecting the crew. Effective communication within the organization fosters a culture of risk awareness. Employees at all levels should feel empowered to communicate potential risks and contribute to the ongoing improvement of risk mitigation measures.

Adaptability and Resilience

Envision adaptability as the crew's ability to adjust sails in changing winds. Organizations must cultivate adaptability and resilience. When unforeseen challenges arise, a flexible and resilient workforce can navigate through adversity and contribute to effective risk mitigation.

Real-world Application: An Organization's Expedition

Imagine an organization planning to launch a new product. This expansion, while promising, comes with inherent risks:

Risk Identification

The organization identifies potential risks, including market competition, supply chain disruptions, and regulatory hurdles. Each of these risks is cataloged based on its nature and potential impact on the new product launch.

Assessment and Prioritization

The organization assesses the potential impact and likelihood of each risk. Market competition is identified as a high-impact risk, given its potential to affect the product's market share. Supply chain disruptions and regulatory hurdles are also prioritized based on their potential consequences.

Mitigation Strategies

Armed with this understanding, the organization develops a risk management plan. Strategies include market research and differentiation to address competition, establishing alternative suppliers to mitigate supply chain risks, and engaging regulatory experts to navigate potential hurdles.

Monitoring and Review

The organization implements continuous monitoring of market dynamics, supply chain health, and regulatory changes. Periodic reviews ensure that the risk management plan remains effective and adaptable to evolving circumstances.

UNDERSTANDING INCIDENT RESPONSE

In the complex realm of cybersecurity, where digital landscapes are dynamic and threats are ever-evolving, understanding incident response is akin to being prepared for the unexpected. Imagine it as having a well-drilled emergency response team ready to spring into action when a security incident occurs, much like a firefighter responding to a sudden blaze. In this exploration, we delve into the human- centric dimensions of incident response, navigating the delicate balance between agility and resilience.

The Prelude: Recognizing the Digital Battlefield

Picture an organization's digital environment as a bustling city, where information flows like traffic, and systems are the lifeblood of daily operations. In this bustling digital city, an incident is like an unexpected disruption—a sudden traffic jam or even a security breach. Understanding incident response begins with recognizing the unique challenges of this digital battlefield.

Identification and Recognition

Consider the identification of an incident as the first responder's call to action. This involves recognizing unusual activities or patterns that could indicate a security incident. It could be the sudden surge in network traffic, an unexpected system outage, or the detection of malicious software.

Categorization and Prioritization

Imagine categorization and prioritization as the dispatcher's role in emergency response. Once an incident is identified, it needs to be categorized based on its nature— whether it's a cyberattack, a system failure, or a data breach. Prioritization follows, determining the severity and potential impact of the incident on the organization's operations.

Crafting the Response: The Human Element in Action

In the face of a security incident, the response is where the human element comes into play. Imagine an incident response team as a squad of skilled firefighters, each with a specific role and a commitment to swiftly and effectively address the situation.

Containment and Eradication

Think of containment and eradication as the firefighters' strategy for controlling and extinguishing a blaze. In incident response, containment involves isolating the affected systems or networks to prevent the incident from spreading. Eradication focuses on removing the root cause of the incident, whether it's a piece of malicious code or a system vulnerability.

Communication and Coordination

Envision communication and coordination as the fire chief's orchestration of resources. Clear communication is crucial during an incident. The incident response team needs to coordinate efforts, share information internally, and communicate with relevant stakeholders, including executives, employees, and possibly law enforcement.

Learning from the Incident

Picture learning from the incident as the post-incident analysis. In the aftermath of a security incident, the incident response team conducts a thorough review. This involves understanding the incident's root cause, assessing the effectiveness of the response, and identifying areas for improvement. Learning from the incident is not just about addressing the immediate threat but also about enhancing the organization's resilience for the future.

Navigating Human Elements: Agility and Resilience

Just as a firefighter must be agile to adapt to changing conditions, an incident response team must navigate through evolving threats with speed and precision.

Agility in Response:

Consider agility in response as the ability to move swiftly in the face of uncertainty. Cyber threats are dynamic and can evolve rapidly. The incident response team must be agile, adapting their strategies and tactics to address the specific characteristics of each incident.

Resilience in Recovery:

Think of resilience in recovery as the firefighter's determination to rebuild after extinguishing a fire. After an incident is contained and eradicated, the focus shifts to recovery. Resilience involves restoring affected systems, assessing the impact on business operations, and implementing measures to prevent similar incidents in the future.

Real-world Application: Cybersecurity Firefighting in Action

Imagine a scenario where a company detects unauthorized access to its customer database. This incident is akin to a security breach—a fire in the digital city. The incident response unfolds as follows:

Identification

The security team identifies the incident through anomaly detection systems that flag unusual access patterns to the customer database.

Categorization and Prioritization

The incident is categorized as a data breach, and its severity is assessed based on the potential compromise of sensitive customer information.

Containment and Eradication

The incident response team swiftly isolates the affected servers to prevent further unauthorized access. They identify and remove the unauthorized accounts and take measures to patch the vulnerability that led to the breach.

Communication and Coordination

The incident response team communicates with the company's executives to provide updates on the incident and coordinates with legal and public relations teams to manage external communication. Affected customers are notified transparently, demonstrating a commitment to accountability.

Learning from the Incident

A post-incident analysis reveals that the breach occurred due to a known vulnerability that hadn't been patched. The incident response team recommends improvements in vulnerability management processes and employee training to prevent similar incidents in the future.

DISASTER RECOVERY PLANNING

In the realm of digital landscapes, where the heartbeat of organizations is their data and systems, disaster recovery planning is akin to crafting a robust insurance policy against the unforeseen. Picture it as a meticulously prepared playbook, ready to be deployed when the unexpected occurs, much like a well-thought-out emergency response plan for a city. In this exploration, we delve into the human-centric dimensions of disaster recovery planning, navigating the delicate balance between prudence and resilience.

Setting the Stage: Recognizing the Vulnerabilities

Imagine an organization's digital infrastructure as a bustling cityscape, with data flowing like the lifeblood of daily operations. In this bustling city, a disaster could be analogous to a sudden blackout—a power outage, a cyberattack, or a catastrophic system failure. Understanding disaster recovery planning begins with recognizing the unique vulnerabilities of this digital metropolis.

Identifying Potential Disasters

Consider identifying potential disasters as the meteorologist's role in predicting storms. This involves recognizing a spectrum of potential disasters, from natural calamities like floods and earthquakes to man-made incidents like cyberattacks, hardware failures, or even human errors.

Assessing the Critical Infrastructure

Imagine assessing the critical infrastructure as the city planner's evaluation of essential services. In the digital realm, critical infrastructure includes servers, databases, communication networks, and the applications that are vital for the organization's operations. Recognizing their importance is crucial for effective disaster recovery planning.

Crafting the Plan: A Human-Centric Approach

In the face of a disaster, a well-crafted disaster recovery plan serves as the community's emergency response, ensuring that services can be restored, and normalcy regained. Picture it as a collective effort, involving various stakeholders coming together to safeguard the city.

Risk Assessment and Prioritization

Think of risk assessment and prioritization as the city's preparedness strategy. The disaster recovery team assesses the potential impact of various disasters and prioritizes them based on severity and likelihood. This ensures that resources are allocated efficiently to address the most critical threats.

Defining Recovery Objectives

Imagine defining recovery objectives as the community's vision for reconstruction. The disaster recovery plan outlines specific objectives, such as the time it should take to restore critical systems and services. This provides a roadmap for the recovery efforts, setting clear expectations for the entire community.

Building Redundancies and Backups

Think of building redundancies and backups as constructing resilient buildings and infrastructure. In the digital landscape, this involves creating duplicate systems, implementing regular data backups, and establishing failover mechanisms. These redundancies ensure that even if one part of the infrastructure is affected, there are alternative pathways for continuity.

Navigating Human Elements: Collaboration and Communication

In the dynamic landscape of disaster recovery planning, collaboration and communication are the lifelines. Just as a community must rally together during a crisis, an organization's disaster recovery team must navigate through challenges with transparency and coordination.

Collaboration across Teams

Consider collaboration across teams as the city's collaborative emergency response. Disaster recovery planning involves multiple teams—IT, security, operations, and management—working together seamlessly. Each team has a unique role in the recovery efforts, and effective collaboration ensures a holistic approach.

Clear Communication Protocols

Think of clear communication protocols as the city's public announcements during a disaster. Communication is paramount in disaster recovery planning. The plan outlines communication protocols, ensuring that stakeholders are informed promptly, internally and externally, about the incident, response efforts, and expected timelines for recovery.

Real-world Application: Recovering from a Cyber Hurricane

Imagine a scenario where a company faces a widespread cyberattack—an incident analogous to a digital hurricane. The disaster recovery plan unfolds as follows:

Identification

The cybersecurity team identifies a sophisticated malware attack affecting critical systems, with the potential to disrupt operations and compromise sensitive data.

Assessment and Prioritization

The incident response team assesses the severity of the attack and prioritizes it as a high-impact incident. The potential consequences include data breaches, operational disruptions, and reputational damage.

Containment and Eradication

The disaster recovery team swiftly isolates affected systems, containing the spread of the malware. They work to eradicate the malicious code, employing cybersecurity measures to neutralize the threat.

Communication and Coordination

The incident is communicated transparently to internal stakeholders, including employees, and external stakeholders, such as customers and regulatory bodies. The disaster recovery team coordinates with cybersecurity experts, legal teams, and public relations to ensure a cohesive and well-informed response.

Recovery and Learning

After containment, the focus shifts to recovery. Backup systems are activated, and redundant processes come into play. A post-incident analysis identifies areas for improvement, such as enhancing cybersecurity measures and conducting employee training to prevent future incidents.

BUSINESS CONTINUITY PLANNING

Business Continuity Planning (BCP) is a proactive strategy for ensuring that an organization's vital operations and delivery of essential products or services can continue in the face of various disruptions or crises. It entails developing and implementing strategies, procedures, and policies to reduce the impact of potential hazards and allow the business to recover swiftly and effectively. We will look at the essential components and actions involved in business continuity planning in this section.

Risk Assessment and Business Impact Analysis

Conducting a complete risk assessment and business impact analysis is the first stage in business continuity planning. This includes assessing potential threats and hazards, such as natural disasters, cyber-attacks, pandemics, or power outages, that could disrupt routine operations. A business impact study also assists in assessing the potential effects of these disruptions on essential processes, resources, and stakeholders. This research lays the groundwork for the development of successful mitigation solutions.

Business Continuity Plan Development

After identifying the risks and potential consequences, the next step is to create a business continuity strategy. This plan outlines the strategies, procedures, and resources needed to keep or restore critical business functions during and after a disruption. Clear roles and duties, communication methods, backup systems, and recovery strategies should all be included in the strategy. Alternative sites, supply chain linkages, and IT infrastructure requirements should all be considered. All essential stakeholders should have access to the plan, which should be documented.

Crisis Management and Response

Crisis management and response tactics should be included in business continuity planning. This entails putting together a crisis management team and specifying their roles and duties. The team should be prepared to respond effectively in the event of a crisis, which includes activating the business continuity plan, coordinating emergency response operations, and communicating with internal and external stakeholders. To ensure fast and accurate distribution of information, crisis communication protocols should be in place.

Backup and Recovery Systems

Backup and recovery solutions are an essential component of business continuity planning. Regular data backups, offsite storage, redundant IT systems, and alternative communication channels are all part of this. To set acceptable downtime and data loss levels, organizations should develop recovery time objectives (RTO) and recovery point objectives (RPO). Backup and recovery systems must be tested and validated on a regular basis to ensure their effectiveness during a real disruption.

Training and Awareness

Employee training and awareness are required for an effective business continuity plan. Employees should be familiarized with their roles and duties during a crisis through regular training sessions and simulations. This comprises procedures for emergency evacuation, communication protocols, and the utilization of backup systems. Awareness programs can help to build a preparation culture and ensure that staff understands the value of business continuity planning.

Testing and Exercising

It is critical to test and exercise the business continuity plan in order to discover any gaps or weaknesses and update the plan accordingly. This can include tabletop exercises, simulation exercises, or full-scale drills to evaluate the success of the strategy and the crisis management team's response. Lessons obtained from these activities should be documented and used to continuously update and improve the plan.

Continuous Monitoring and Improvement

Business continuity planning is a continual activity that necessitates constant monitoring and improvement. Periodic reviews and updates should be conducted by organizations to reflect changes in the business climate, technology, or risk landscape. This includes revising the risk assessment, updating contact information, assessing recovery strategies, and applying lessons learned from real-world occurrences or exercises.

Organizations can reduce the effect of disruptions and assure the continuity of important activities by adopting a solid business continuity plan. It enables them to respond to emergencies effectively, protect their employees and stakeholders, maintain customer trust, and ensure their long-term profitability.

How to prepare for unexpected events

Preparing for unanticipated events necessitates a proactive and comprehensive approach that encompasses all parts of a company, including people, technology, and operations. Organizations can improve their readiness and resilience to deal with unexpected events by employing the following measures:

Risk Assessment and Scenario Planning

Conduct an in-depth risk assessment to identify potential hazards and their impact on various sections of the organization. Natural disasters, cybersecurity threats, supply chain disruptions, and public health concerns should all be considered in this assessment. Create scenarios based on these risks to better understand how they might play out and the potential repercussions. This data will serve as the foundation for future preparedness activities.

Business Continuity Planning

Create a detailed business continuity plan outlining the measures to be done in the case of an unforeseen incident. This strategy should contain measures for keeping critical processes running smoothly, ensuring employee safety, and communicating with stakeholders. During a crisis, identify vital functions, build backup systems and other locations, and specify roles and duties for key individuals. Review and update the plan on a regular basis to handle emerging risks and changing conditions.

Cross-Functional Training and Awareness

Provide training and awareness initiatives to staff at all levels and departments within the firm. Educate them on potential hazards, emergency response processes, and their roles and duties in the case of an unforeseen event. Create a preparedness culture and encourage staff to disclose any potential dangers or vulnerabilities they discover. Regular drills and simulations should be conducted to assess the effectiveness of preparedness measures and identify areas for improvement.

Communication and Crisis Management

Create a strong communication strategy for internal and external stakeholders during unforeseen situations. Define the communication channels, key spokespersons, and escalation procedures in detail. Make certain that all staff are aware of the communication protocols and have access to up-to-date contact information. To ensure consistent and timely communication, create pre-approved messages and templates for various scenarios. Monitor news and social media outlets to respond to disinformation as soon as possible.

Technology and Data Protection

Examine the organization's IT infrastructure and data security procedures to ensure they are resilient to unforeseen circumstances. To protect sensitive information, implement backup systems, data recovery procedures, and cybersecurity protocols. Update and test IT systems on a regular basis to uncover vulnerabilities and rectify any potential flaws. To ensure business continuity during a crisis, consider cloud-based solutions and remote access capabilities.

Supply Chain and Vendor Management

Examine and diversify the organization's supply chain to reduce disruptions caused by unanticipated incidents. Determine important suppliers and develop alternate sources or backup plans. Establish partnerships with secondary vendors to assure the availability of critical goods and services. Assess the financial health and risk profile of major vendors on a regular basis to mitigate supply chain risks. To be aware of potential disruptions, establish clear contact routes with suppliers.

Insurance and Risk Transfer

Collaborate with insurance providers to assess the organization's insurance coverage and ensure it is enough for any hazards. Consider purchasing additional coverage or adding riders to meet specific risks connected with unforeseen situations. Investigate risk- transfer possibilities via contractual agreements, such as indemnification clauses or force majeure provisions. Consult with legal professionals to better grasp the organization's liabilities and obligations in various scenarios.

Continuous Monitoring and Evaluation

Create a system for ongoing monitoring and evaluation of preparedness measures. Based on changing circumstances and developing risks, review and update risk assessments, business continuity plans, and communication protocols on a regular basis. Conduct post- event evaluations to identify key takeaways and areas for improvement. Stay informed about best practices and new trends in preparedness by connecting with industry networks, government agencies, and professional groups.

Organizations can improve their ability to navigate unforeseen occurrences by taking a proactive and integrated approach to preparedness. Remember that readiness is a continuous activity that involves continual review, adaption, and participation from all levels of the organization.

While organizations seek to monitor and predict various hazards, certain aspects can be difficult, if not impossible, to monitor and predict effectively. These uncertainties might represent serious dangers to a company. Let us look at a few examples:

Black Swan Events

Black swan events are unusual, unexpected events with catastrophic consequences that are impossible to predict using traditional forecasting methods. Natural disasters, economic crises, and technology disruptions are examples of unexpected events that can have far-reaching implications. Organizations may find it difficult to anticipate and plan for such disasters due to their unpredictable nature.

Rapid Technological Advancements

Technology is advancing at an unprecedented rate, bringing with it new hazards and opportunities. It can be difficult to predict the precise direction and impact of technological developments such as artificial intelligence, blockchain, or quantum computing. Organizations may find it difficult to predict how these advances may disrupt industries, introduce new dangers, or transform business strategies.

Regulatory Changes

Governments and regulatory agencies frequently enact new laws, regulations, or policies that have far-reaching consequences for industries and organizations. It might be difficult to predict the timing, extent, or specifics of regulatory changes. Organizations may encounter compliance risks or obstacles while modifying their operations to meet new regulations, particularly in industries with complex or rapidly changing regulatory environments.

Global Geopolitical Events

Political insecurity, economic disputes, and geopolitical crises can all have a significant influence on enterprises that operate in numerous nations. These occurrences are frequently unpredictable, and their outcomes can be unpredictable. Changes in government policy, trade obstacles, or societal instability in diverse locations may pose hazards to organizations with international operations.

Emerging Risks

As the world changes, new dangers develop that businesses may not have encountered previously. Examples include cybersecurity concerns, climate change-related hazards, and social media-related reputational risks. Because of their dynamic nature and the lack of previous data or existing risk management frameworks, identifying and assessing emerging risks can be difficult.

Human Behavior and Psychology

Human behavior and psychology can be complicated and unpredictable, presenting hazards that are difficult to quantify and successfully monitor. Employee misconduct, consumer sentiment, and public opinion can all have a substantial impact on a company's reputation and performance. Predicting and controlling risks associated with human behavior necessitates a thorough grasp of social dynamics as well as individual decision- making processes.

While these uncertainties pose difficulties, organizations can nevertheless take proactive actions to mitigate the risks associated with them:

1. Develop a Resilient and Agile Culture
Create a company culture that values flexibility, resilience, and agility. This will allow the company to adapt to unforeseen events and manage uncertain situations more successfully.

2. Scenario Planning and Contingency Strategies
Participate in scenario planning exercises to investigate several potential future scenarios and establish contingency plans. This enables companies to be better prepared to respond to and adapt to unforeseen circumstances.

3. Foster a Learning Culture
Encourage internal knowledge-sharing and constant learning. This allows employees to stay up to date on developing trends and threats, allowing the firm to adapt and respond more effectively.

4. Diversification and Redundancy
To mitigate the impact of unforeseen occurrences in specific regions or industries, consider diversifying activities, supply lines, or markets. Adding redundancy to important systems and processes can also help to reduce the risks associated with technical breakdowns or disruptions.

5. Collaboration and Information Sharing

Create networks and collaborations with other organizations, industry associations, or governmental authorities to share information and collaborate on risk monitoring and management activities. Collective intelligence and shared resources can assist in more effectively addressing uncertainties.

It is critical to recognize that complete eradication of ambiguity is not achievable. Organizations, on the other hand, can improve their resilience and ability to respond to unforeseen events and uncertainties by taking a proactive and flexible approach to risk management.

Chapter 10

ETHICAL AND LEGAL CONSIDERATIONS

UNDERSTANDING ETHICAL AND LEGAL CONSIDERATIONS IN CYBERSECURITY

In this section, we navigate the human-centric dimensions of ethical and legal considerations in cybersecurity, threading the delicate balance between innovation and responsibility.

Setting the Stage: The Intersection of Ethics and Law

Picture the digital realm as a bustling metropolis, with data flowing like the lifeblood of daily interactions. In this vibrant city, ethical considerations are the unwritten rules that guide behavior, and legal frameworks are the established laws that maintain order. Understanding ethical and legal considerations in cybersecurity begins with acknowledging the intricacies of this intersection.

Defining Ethical Boundaries

Consider defining ethical boundaries as the community's collective agreement on right and wrong. In the digital landscape, ethical considerations involve questions of privacy, consent, and the responsible use of technology. Defining these boundaries is essential to ensure that technological advancements align with societal values.

Navigating Legal Frameworks

Imagine navigating legal frameworks as understanding the city's laws and regulations. In the cybersecurity realm, legal considerations encompass a spectrum of regulations governing data protection, intellectual property, and cybercrime. Navigating these frameworks is crucial to ensure that organizations operate within the bounds of the law.

Crafting a Responsible Approach: A Human- Centric Perspective

In the face of technological advancements, crafting a responsible approach to cybersecurity involves recognizing the impact of actions on individuals, communities, and societies at large. It's akin to urban planning, where the city's architects consider the well-being of its inhabitants.

Respecting User Privacy

Think of respecting user privacy as ensuring that individuals can move through the digital city without constant surveillance. Ethical considerations in cybersecurity demand a respect for user privacy, requiring organizations to be transparent about data collection practices, seek informed consent, and prioritize the security of personal information.

Ensuring Data Security

Imagine ensuring data security as constructing robust buildings to withstand potential threats. Both ethically and legally, organizations have a responsibility to safeguard the data entrusted to them. This involves implementing secure practices, encryption measures, and proactive measures to prevent data breaches.

Transparent Communication

Think of transparent communication as the city's public announcements during a crisis. In both ethical and legal contexts, clear communication is paramount. Organizations must be transparent about their cybersecurity practices, inform users about potential risks, and provide updates on security measures in place.

Navigating Human Elements: Responsibility and Accountability

In the digital metropolis, the principles of responsibility and accountability are the cornerstones of ethical and legal considerations. Just as a city's residents are accountable for their actions, organizations must navigate through the complex web of technology with a sense of responsibility.

Educating and Empowering Users

Consider educating and empowering users as fostering an informed citizenry. Ethically, organizations should invest in user education, ensuring that individuals understand the risks associated with their digital activities. This empowerment enables users to make informed decisions about their online presence.

Legal Compliance and Due Diligence

Imagine legal compliance and due diligence as adhering to the city's building codes and safety regulations. Organizations have a legal responsibility to comply with relevant cybersecurity regulations. This involves conducting due diligence, staying informed about evolving laws, and adapting cybersecurity practices accordingly.

Real-world Application: Cybersecurity in the Digital City

Imagine a scenario where a technology company develops a new application that collects extensive user data for personalized services. Ethical and legal considerations come into play:

Ethical Boundaries

The company, in defining ethical boundaries, prioritizes user privacy. It provides clear information about data collection practices, obtains informed consent from users, and allows them to opt out of certain data-sharing features. This ethical approach ensures that users' rights and choices are respected.

Legal Compliance

Navigating legal frameworks, the company ensures compliance with data protection regulations. It conducts regular privacy impact assessments, updates its policies in response to legal changes, and maintains a transparent record of its data processing activities. Legal compliance becomes an integral part of the company's operations.

Responsibility and Accountability

Taking a responsible approach, the company invests in user education programs. It informs users about cybersecurity best practices, educates them about potential risks, and empowers them to take control of their digital security. This proactive stance aligns with both ethical and legal considerations.

CYBERCRIME LAWS AND REGULATIONS

In the vast landscape of the digital world, where the interconnected web of technology intertwines with human behavior, the need for cybercrime laws and regulations becomes paramount. Imagine this landscape as a bustling cityscape, where digital citizens engage in activities that mirror their real-world counterparts, and where laws and regulations serve as the framework for maintaining order and safeguarding individuals and organizations. In this exploration, we navigate the human-centric dimensions of cybercrime laws and regulations, threading the delicate balance between technological innovation and legal responsibility.

Setting the Stage: The Digital City and Its Inhabitants

Picture the digital realm as a bustling city, where individuals, businesses, and governments engage in various activities. In this city, cybercrime laws and regulations are the legal infrastructure designed to protect citizens and maintain the integrity of digital interactions. Understanding this legal framework begins with acknowledging the complexities of the digital city.

Defining Cybercrime

Consider defining cybercrime as identifying illicit activities within the digital city. Cybercrime encompasses a wide range of offenses, including unauthorized access to systems, data breaches, identity theft, online fraud, and the dissemination of malware. Defining these crimes is crucial for creating laws that can effectively address them.

Protecting Digital Citizens

Imagine protecting digital citizens as the city's commitment to ensuring the safety of its inhabitants. Cybercrime laws and regulations are designed to safeguard individuals and organizations from malicious activities. This involves creating legal boundaries that deter cybercriminals and hold them accountable for their actions.

Crafting Legal Safeguards: A Human-Centric Approach

In the face of technological advancements, crafting legal safeguards against cybercrime involves recognizing the impact of digital offenses on individuals, businesses, and societies. It's akin to drafting laws that protect citizens from harm in the physical world.

Defining Offenses and Penalties

Think of defining offenses and penalties as outlining the consequences for breaking digital laws. Cybercrime laws specify what constitutes illegal activities, such as hacking, data theft, or online fraud. These laws also delineate the penalties for offenders, ranging from fines to imprisonment, depending on the severity of the crime.

Addressing Jurisdictional Challenges

Imagine addressing jurisdictional challenges as creating laws that transcend digital borders. Cybercrimes often transcend national boundaries, making it challenging to prosecute offenders. Effective laws need to account for these challenges, fostering international cooperation and collaboration among law enforcement agencies.

Protecting Privacy and Digital Rights

Think of protecting privacy and digital rights as upholding the city's commitment to individual freedoms. Cybercrime laws should include provisions that protect individuals' privacy and digital rights, ensuring that law enforcement actions respect these fundamental aspects even in the digital space.

Navigating Human Elements: Awareness and Enforcement

In the digital city, the principles of awareness and enforcement are crucial. Just as citizens need to be aware of laws in the physical world, digital citizens must understand cybercrime laws, and enforcement mechanisms must be robust to deter offenders.

Public Awareness and Education

Consider public awareness and education as empowering citizens with knowledge. Effective cybercrime laws are complemented by educational programs that inform individuals about the risks of cybercrime, how to protect themselves online, and the legal implications of engaging in malicious activities.

Law Enforcement Training

Imagine law enforcement training as equipping the city's guardians with the skills needed to combat digital threats. Cybercrime laws are most effective when law enforcement agencies are well-trained in investigating and prosecuting offenses. This involves staying abreast of technological advancements and understanding the evolving tactics of cybercriminals.

Real-world Application: The Fight against Online Fraud

Imagine a scenario where a financial institution faces a surge in online fraud—digital pickpocketing. The application of cyber-crime laws unfolds as follows:

Defining Online Fraud

Cybercrime laws clearly define online fraud as the unauthorized use of digital means to deceive individuals or organizations for financial gain. This includes activities such as phishing, identity theft, and fraudulent online schemes.

Penalties for Offenders

The laws outline specific penalties for individuals found guilty of online fraud, ranging from fines to imprisonment, depending on the scale and impact of the fraudulent activities. These penalties act as deterrents, discouraging potential offenders.

International Cooperation

Recognizing that online fraud often involves perpetrators operating across borders, the legal framework includes provisions for international cooperation. This involves collaboration between law enforcement agencies from different countries to investigate and apprehend offenders.

Protecting Victims' Rights

Cybercrime laws include provisions that protect the rights of victims of online fraud. This includes mechanisms for reporting incidents, seeking restitution, and ensuring that victims are not unjustly penalized for offenses committed by perpetrators using their identities.

PROFESSIONAL AND ETHICAL RESPONSIBILITIES

In the dynamic landscape of professional life, where individuals navigate their careers and contribute to various fields, the concepts of professional and ethical responsibilities form the bedrock of a conscientious and accountable workforce. Picture this landscape as a diverse and bustling city, where professionals from different domains collaborate and innovate. In this exploration, we delve into the human- centric dimensions of professional and ethical responsibilities, threading the delicate balance between career aspirations and moral integrity.

Setting the Stage: The Professional City and Its Inhabitants

Imagine the professional world as a thriving cityscape, where individuals pursue careers, collaborate on projects, and contribute to the development of their respective fields. In this city, professional responsibilities are the unwritten rules that guide behavior, and ethical considerations serve as the moral compass that ensures integrity in decision-making.

Defining Professional Responsibilities

Consider defining professional responsibilities as recognizing the duties and obligations that come with a chosen career path. Just as each occupation contributes uniquely to the overall functioning of the professional city, professionals have specific responsibilities tied to their roles, whether it's delivering quality work, meeting deadlines, or upholding industry standards.

Embracing Ethical Considerations

Imagine embracing ethical considerations as acknowledging the importance of moral principles in professional life. Ethical responsibilities transcend the specific tasks associated with a job and involve considerations of honesty, transparency, and fairness. Professionals, like citizens in a city, must navigate through their careers with a sense of ethical awareness.

Crafting a Conscientious Approach: A Human-Centric Perspective

In the face of diverse professional challenges, crafting a conscientious approach to professional and ethical responsibilities involves recognizing the impact of individual actions on colleagues, organizations, and society at large. It's akin to urban planning, where the well-being of citizens is central to the city's design.

Delivering Quality Work

Think of delivering quality work as contributing to the city's infrastructure. Just as sturdy buildings ensure the stability of a city, professionals are responsible for delivering work that meets or exceeds industry standards. This involves continuous learning, skill development, and a commitment to excellence.

Meeting Deadlines and Commitments

Imagine meeting deadlines and commitments as ensuring the smooth flow of activities in the city. In the professional realm, adhering to timelines and fulfilling commitments is crucial for maintaining trust and reliability. This responsibility extends to collaborating effectively with colleagues to achieve shared goals.

Maintaining Professional Integrity

Think of maintaining professional integrity as upholding the city's code of conduct. Professionals are entrusted with confidential information and must act with integrity in all interactions. This involves avoiding conflicts of interest, being honest in communications, and respecting the intellectual property of others.

Navigating Human Elements: Collaboration and Empathy

In the professional city, the principles of collaboration and empathy are crucial. Just as citizens in a city work together for common goals, professionals must navigate through their careers with a sense of teamwork and understanding.

Collaboration across Professions

Consider collaboration across professions as the city's collaborative efforts in times of need. Professionals often work in interdisciplinary teams, each contributing their expertise to solve complex problems. Effective collaboration requires open communication, mutual respect, and an appreciation for diverse perspectives.

Empathy in the Workplace

Imagine empathy in the workplace as fostering a supportive community within the city. Professionals must be attuned to the well-being of their colleagues, understanding the pressures and challenges they may face. This involves cultivating a workplace culture that values mental health, inclusivity, and a sense of belonging.

Real-world Application: Ethical Leadership in a Corporate City

Imagine a scenario where a corporate leader faces a decision about the release of a new product that has potential safety concerns. Ethical leadership, guided by professional responsibilities, comes into play:

Quality and Safety Considerations

The leader, recognizing their professional responsibility for delivering quality products, conducts thorough assessments of the potential safety issues associated with the product. This involves engaging with relevant experts, conducting rigorous testing, and ensuring that the product meets or exceeds safety standards.

Transparent Communication

Ethical considerations come to the forefront as the leader communicates transparently with stakeholders about the potential safety concerns. This involves providing clear information about the assessments, potential risks, and the steps taken to address the issues. Transparency builds trust and aligns with the ethical responsibility to keep stakeholders informed.

Collaborative Decision-Making

The leader embraces collaborative decision-making, involving key stakeholders, including product development teams, legal experts, and external safety regulators. This collaborative approach ensures that diverse perspectives are considered, ethical concerns are addressed, and decisions are made collectively.

Empathy for Consumers

Ethical leadership extends to empathy for consumers who might be affected by the safety concerns. The leader takes proactive measures to mitigate potential risks, communicates directly with consumers about safety precautions, and demonstrates a genuine concern for their well-being.

Codes of Conduct and Professionalism

A code of conduct is a set of principles that guides the behaviour of an individual or group. Codes of conduct exist in many different professions, and they often outline the standards of behaviour expected from members of the profession.

Many associations have codes of conduct. The ACFE, for example, has the Code of Professional Ethics. The code lays out a set of principles that professionals should follow to maintain the integrity and professionalism of the field. Some key points from the code include:

Honesty and Integrity: Professionals must always act with honesty and integrity in their professional and personal lives.

Confidentiality: Professionals must keep all information obtained during their work confidential. This includes not sharing any information about investigations or clients with unauthorized individuals.

Professionalism: Professionals must always act professionally with clients and other professionals, as well as in their general conduct.

Avoiding Conflicts of Interest: Professionals must avoid any conflicts of interest that could compromise their ability to do their job correctly.

Acting with integrity: You should always act honestly and ethically, even when making tough decisions.

Not engaging in bribery or corruption: It is essential to maintain the public's trust by refusing to engage in illegal activities.

Abiding by the law: You must comply with all applicable laws and regulations governing your sector.

By following these codes of conduct, you can help ensure that you are viewed as a reputable and trustworthy member of your community.

Following these codes of conduct will help you uphold the high standards expected of those in this field. It is also essential to be aware of potential ethical traps that may occur in your work. For example, you may be faced with the decision of whether to report a suspected crime or protect a client. It is crucial to weigh all the factors involved and decide what is best for everyone involved.

Being a responsible and ethical professional can help ensure that this field remains trustworthy and respected.

Why are codes of conduct necessary?

Codes of conduct are essential because they help maintain the integrity and professionalism. They guide members of the profession on acting ethically and responsibly in their work.

When professions have codes of conduct, it helps ensure that everyone involved in that profession behaves responsibly. This can help build trust between professionals and the public. It can also help protect the reputation of the profession as a whole.

It is essential to be familiar with the code of conduct that applies to that field. By following these guidelines, you can help ensure that you always act with integrity and professionalism. This will reflect positively on you and your chosen profession.

What should be included in a code of conduct?

A code of conduct should include a set of principles that members of the profession are expected to follow. These principles should be based on the values and ethics of the profession. They should also be in line with applicable laws and regulations.

When drafting a code of conduct, it is essential to consider all potential ethical traps in a professional's work. For example, you may need to weigh the pros and cons of reporting a suspected crime. It would also help guide how professionals should deal with conflicts of interest.

The code of conduct should be reviewed and updated regularly to reflect the latest changes in law and ethics. It is also essential to communicate the code to all professional members so they know the expectations of them.

How can codes of conduct help with professional development?

A code of conduct can be a valuable tool for professional development by guiding ethical and legal principles. It can also help build trust within the profession and create a culture of accountability. By following a code of conduct, professionals can demonstrate their commitment to upholding high standards of integrity and professionalism. This can make them more attractive to employers and enhance their reputation in the field. Additionally, codes of conduct often provide training resources and support mechanisms, which can be helpful for career growth. Professionals who are interested in developing their skills would do well to explore the codes of conduct relevant to their field.

Professionals need to maintain high standards of ethics and integrity to protect the industry's reputation. A code of conduct can be a valuable tool for achieving this goal. By following the guidelines in a code of conduct, professionals can demonstrate their commitment to upholding the highest standards of integrity and professionalism. This can make them more attractive to employers and enhance their reputation in their field.

Internal accountability

Internal accountability holds employees and organizations responsible for their actions within an organization. This includes everything from financial fraud prevention to money laundering prevention, as well as other financial crimes.

One of the most important aspects of a prevention programme is internal accountability. Everyone in the organization must be aware of their responsibilities and adhere to the established policies and procedures. Management must provide adequate resources, including training, to ensure that employees effectively carry out their duties. It is also critical that individuals who identify potential or actual violations report them promptly to be addressed.

Internal accountability is essential for protecting an organization from losses, but it also helps promote a culture of compliance, reducing the chances of future incidents. By establishing clear lines of responsibility and encouraging employees to raise any concerns, organizations can create an environment where doing the right thing is the norm. This not only benefits the company financially but also helps to protect its reputation.

Why Internal Accountability Matters

A professional's success depends on their ability to maintain a high level of internal accountability. This means adhering to the highest standards of ethics and integrity and being willing to hold themselves accountable for their actions. They can build trust with their colleagues and superiors by doing so, which is essential in this field. Maintaining a strong sense of internal accountability also helps protect them against corruption and other forms of wrongdoing.

Internal accountability is critical in the workplace. It may be even more important in field of cybersecurity, as the potential consequences of misconduct are often much more significant. A professional who fails to uphold the highest standards can do severe damage to their organization and may even be responsible for economic losses.

It is therefore essential for anyone in cyber-related field to maintain a strong sense of internal accountability. By doing so, they can help protect themselves, their colleagues, and their organization from wrongdoing. And that is something we can all agree is essential.

Internal accountability is critical for protecting an organization from financial losses, but it also benefits. By holding employees accountable for their actions, organizations can improve compliance with applicable laws and regulations, reduce the chances of future incidents, and create a culture where doing the right thing is the norm. This not only protects the company financially but also its reputation.

How to Establish an Effective Internal Accountability Programme

There are many ways to establish an effective internal accountability programme. One of the most important things is to have clear lines of responsibility and encourage employees to raise any concerns. Organizations can also promote a culture of compliance by establishing standards of conduct and providing training on identifying potential crimes.

It is also essential to have a system in place to investigate allegations of misconduct and hold those responsible accountable. This helps ensure that anyone who commits wrongdoing will be held accountable and sends a message that such behaviour will not be tolerated.

Establishing an effective internal accountability programme takes time and effort, but it is well worth it in the long run. By doing so, you can help protect your organization from losses and create a culture of compliance.

The Benefits of a Strong Internal Accountability Programme

When it comes to preventing and investigating potential crimes, having a solid internal accountability programme is vital. This means that your company has in place systems and procedures that hold employees accountable for their actions. Such a system can help deter crime and identify and investigate any criminal activity.

A robust internal accountability programme should include the following:
- Clear policies and procedures detailing what is expected of employees

- Appropriate training on how to recognize and report crime
- Robust reporting mechanisms, including hotlines for employees to report suspicious activity anonymously
- Frequent audits to ensure compliance with policies and procedures
- Improved compliance with applicable laws and regulations
- Reduced chances of future incidents
- A culture where doing the right thing is the norm

These benefits are essential, but the last one is perhaps the most important – a culture where doing the right thing is the norm. When employees feel like they will be held accountable for their actions, they are less likely to engage in misconduct. This helps protect not just the organization financially but also its reputation. Establishing an effective internal accountability programme is one of the best ways to create such a culture.

Tips for Implementing and Maintaining Your Successful Programme

So, how do you implement and maintain your own successful internal accountability programme? Here are a few tips:
- **Start with the basics.** Ensure that your policies and procedures are clear and concise and that employees have adequate training to recognize and report concerns
- **Use effective reporting mechanisms.** Hotlines are an excellent way to encourage employees to report suspicious activity anonymously, without fear of reprisal.
- **Conduct frequent audits.** Audits help ensure compliance with policies and procedures and applicable laws and regulations.

- **Encourage employee engagement.** Promote a culture where doing the right thing is the norm by holding managers accountable for their team's actions, celebrating whistle-blowers, etc.

By following these tips, you can create and maintain a successful internal accountability programme that will help protect your organization from crime.

External accountability

External accountability is a system in which an organization is answerable to outside parties for its actions. This can include government entities, customers, or other interested groups. External accountability can help ensure that organizations act ethically and in the best interests of their stakeholders.

One of the most critical aspects of external accountability is transparency. Organizations should be open and honest about their activities, and they should be willing to share information with those who have a stake in them. This includes making financial reports available, disclosing details on investigations, and explaining decisions made by the organization.

External accountability can help organizations stay out of trouble, but it can also help improve them. When stakeholders are aware of what an organization is doing, they can provide feedback that can help the organization improve its operations. This type of feedback can be precious for organizations working to address unethical behaviour or crimes.

Organizations that embrace external accountability will likely find themselves better positioned to succeed both ethically and financially.

The benefits of external accountability

Many professionals work in isolation and may not have regular contact with their peers. While this can be beneficial for creativity and problem solving, it can also lead to a lack of external accountability. This can be dangerous, leading to complacency and a feeling of invincibility. Therefore, professionals can benefit from having a strong network of colleagues that they can turn to for advice and feedback. A professional organization or trade association can be a great way to connect with other professionals, exchange ideas, and learn from others' experiences.

There are many benefits to external accountability, including:

Improved ethical behaviour: When professionals are held accountable by their peers, they are more likely to act ethically and follow the law.

Better financial performance: When professionals are held accountable, they are more likely to take their work seriously and make sure that they meet all the requirements expected of them.

Reduced risk of fraud: When individuals know that others monitor their actions, they are less likely to engage in fraudulent behaviour.

Greater transparency: When individuals and organizations are held accountable, it leads to greater transparency and helps to prevent corruption.

Results in more practical studies: When professionals are aware that their actions are being monitored, they are less likely to engage in criminal activity. This can help to improve the overall quality of investigations.

Stronger relationships with stakeholders: One of the critical goals of professionals is to build strong relationships with their stakeholders. When professionals are held accountable, it can help to strengthen these relationships and improve communication between all parties involved.

Each of these benefits is important in its own individual way, but they all work together to create a strong foundation for an organization. When organizations embrace external accountability, they become more accountable to their stakeholders and also improve their operations. This leads to a better reputation for the organization, which can help it achieve its goals both ethically and financially.

Types of organizations that can provide external accountability

Many different types of organizations can provide external responsibility for financial crime professionals. Some of the most common include:

Professional organizations: One of the best ways to connect with other professionals is through an industry organization. These organizations offer a variety of resources, including networking opportunities, educational programmes, and job boards. Many professional organizations also have ethics codes that members must abide by.

Trade associations: Trade associations are another great way to connect with others in your field. They typically offer various beneficial services, including education, advocacy, and networking events. Trade associations can also help develop industry-specific knowledge.

Regulatory agencies: Regulatory agencies play an essential role in holding individuals and organizations accountable. They are responsible for enforcing regulations and investigating allegations of wrongdoing. Regulatory agencies can provide several resources, including guidance documents, training programmes, and information about investigations.

Professional review organizations: Professional review organizations are another option for professionals who want to be held accountable. These organizations evaluate the performance of individual professionals and offer feedback. This can help professionals improve their skills and make sure that they comply with applicable laws and regulations.

Each of these options has its benefits, so it is essential to choose one that fits your needs. Professional organizations, trade associations, and regulatory agencies are all excellent choices for connecting with others in their field. If you are looking for more formal accountability, then professional review organizations may be a good option for you. Whichever route you choose, make sure that the organization is reputable and has a robust code of ethics.

External accountability is an essential part of any crime prevention strategy. When individuals and organizations are held accountable, it leads to greater transparency and helps to prevent corruption. Additionally, more effective investigations can be conducted when professionals know that their actions are being monitored. Finally, stronger relationships with stakeholders can be developed when professionals are held accountable. Each of these benefits is important in its way, and they all work together to create a strong foundation for an organization. Choose an external accountability option that fits your needs and get started today!

How to choose an organization for external accountability

When looking for an organization to provide external accountability, you should consider a few things. First, make sure that the organization is reputable, respected and has a strong code of ethics. Second, determine what type of services the organization offers. Third, decide what kind of support you need from the organization. Fourth, ask if the organization has any resources that could be helpful for you, such as training programmes or guidance documents. Finally, find out how much the organization costs to be involved with and whether discounts are available.

Choosing an external accountability option can be difficult, but it is essential to do your research before deciding. Many different organizations offer various services, so take your time and find one that fits your needs.

The steps involved in setting up a relationship with an organization for external accountability

Once you have chosen an organization for external accountability, the next step is to set up a relationship with them. This usually involves signing a contract and paying any associated fees. In some cases, you may also be required to provide certain information or documents.

The process of setting up a relationship can vary from organization to organization, so it is essential to read the instructions carefully. Make sure that you understand what is expected of you and how the relationship will work. If there are any questions, do not hesitate to contact the organization's customer service department.

Setting up a relationship with an external accountability organization is essential in creating a solid crime prevention strategy. By working with an established organization, you can ensure that your team has access to the latest information and resources. Additionally, you will be held accountable to high standards of ethics and professionalism.

Chapter 11

EMERGING THREATS
AND TRENDS

UNDERSTANDING EMERGING CYBERSECURITY THREATS AND TRENDS

Consider defining emerging threats as identifying the potential risks and challenges that evolve in the ever- changing digital city. These threats can take various forms, from sophisticated cyber-attacks and Ransomware to social engineering tactics aimed at exploiting human vulnerabilities. Defining these threats is crucial for developing effective cybersecurity strategies.

Navigating Technological Trends

Imagine navigating technological trends as understanding the city's ever-changing skyline. Just as new buildings reshape the cityscape, technological trends shape the digital landscape. These trends include advancements in artificial intelligence, cloud computing, and the Internet of Things (IoT). Navigating these trends is essential for staying ahead of potential cybersecurity challenges.

Crafting a Resilient Approach: A Human- Centric Perspective

In the face of technological advancements and evolving threats, crafting a resilient approach to emerging cybersecurity threats involves recognizing the impact on individuals, organizations, and societies. It's akin to urban planning, where the city's architects design infrastructure that can withstand unforeseen challenges.

Adapting to Advanced Cyberattacks

Think of adapting to advanced cyberattacks as fortifying the city against new and sophisticated threats. Cybercriminals continually refine their tactics, utilizing advanced techniques to breach security measures. Organizations must adapt by investing in advanced cybersecurity solutions, threat intelligence, and employee training to recognize and thwart these evolving threats.

Securing the Internet of Things (IoT)

Imagine securing the Internet of Things as ensuring the safety of smart devices in the city. The proliferation of IoT devices introduces new vulnerabilities, as these interconnected devices become potential entry points for cyberattacks. A resilient approach involves implementing robust security measures for IoT devices and establishing protocols for secure communication.

Addressing Social Engineering

Think of addressing social engineering as fostering a community that is resilient against manipulation. Social engineering exploits human psychology to trick individuals into divulging sensitive information. A human-centric approach involves educating individuals about common social engineering tactics, promoting awareness, and implementing security measures that minimize the risk of falling victim to such attacks.

Navigating Human Elements: Cybersecurity Awareness and Collaboration

In the digital city, the principles of cybersecurity awareness and collaboration are crucial. Just as citizens in a city work together for common goals, digital citizens must navigate through the digital landscape with a sense of cybersecurity awareness and collaborative efforts.

Promoting Cybersecurity Awareness

Consider promoting cybersecurity awareness as informing citizens about potential risks in the city. Cybersecurity awareness programs are essential for educating individuals about the latest threats, best practices for digital hygiene, and the importance of reporting suspicious activities. Awareness empowers digital citizens to be proactive in their cybersecurity practices.

Collaboration across Sectors

Imagine collaboration across sectors as different communities within the city coming together to address shared challenges. Cybersecurity threats often affect multiple sectors, and collaboration among government agencies, private enterprises, and cybersecurity experts is essential. Information sharing and joint efforts contribute to a more secure digital ecosystem.

Real-world Application: Defending against Ransomware Attacks

Imagine a scenario where a city faces a surge in Ransomware attacks, threatening critical infrastructure and services. A resilient approach unfolds as follows:

Advanced Threat Detection

In response to evolving Ransomware tactics, the city invests in advanced threat detection solutions that can identify and neutralize Ransomware before it can cause damage. This involves leveraging machine learning algorithms and behavioral analytics to detect anomalous patterns indicative of a Ransomware attack.

Collaborative Incident Response

Recognizing that Ransomware attacks can have widespread consequences, the city establishes a collaborative incident response framework. Different agencies and organizations work together to share threat intelligence, coordinate response efforts, and collectively mitigate the impact of Ransomware incidents.

Public Awareness Campaigns

The city launches public awareness campaigns to educate citizens and employees about the risks of Ransomware and how to recognize phishing attempts. This includes providing resources for secure data backup practices and emphasizing the importance of reporting suspicious emails or activities.

Engaging with the Private Sector

The city collaborates with private enterprises that may be targeted by Ransomware attacks. This includes critical infrastructure providers, healthcare organizations, and financial institutions. Joint efforts involve sharing threat intelligence, conducting joint training exercises, and implementing security measures to collectively enhance resilience.

CLOUD SECURITY

In the expansive realm of digital technology, where the cloud looms large as a transformative force, cloud security stands as the gatekeeper, safeguarding the vast troves of data and services that float within this virtual expanse. Picture the cloud as a city in the sky, with data and applications soaring through the digital stratosphere. In this exploration, we navigate the human-centric dimensions of cloud security, threading the delicate balance between the convenience of cloud computing and the imperative to fortify against potential risks.

Setting the Scene: The Cloud City and Its Inhabitants

Imagine the cloud as a bustling city in the sky, where individuals, businesses, and institutions store their digital lives and conduct myriad activities. In this city, cloud security becomes the protective shield, ensuring the confidentiality, integrity, and availability of data and services. Understanding this landscape begins with acknowledging the complexities of the Cloud City.

Defining Cloud Security

Consider defining cloud security as the set of measures designed to safeguard data, applications, and infrastructure in the cloud. Just as a city has walls and gates for protection, cloud security involves protocols and technologies that shield against unauthorized access, data breaches, and other cyber threats. Defining these security measures is paramount for building trust in cloud services.

Navigating Shared Responsibility

Imagine navigating shared responsibility as understanding that the Cloud City is a collaborative effort between cloud service providers and their users. Cloud providers ensure the security of the cloud, including the physical infrastructure and underlying services, while users are responsible in the cloud, managing the security of their data and applications. This shared responsibility model forms the cornerstone of cloud security.

Crafting a Secure Skyline: A Human-Centric Perspective

In the face of diverse digital challenges, crafting a secure skyline in the Cloud City involves recognizing the impact of individual and collective actions on data privacy, user trust, and the overall stability of the cloud. It's akin to urban planning, where architects design structures with the safety and well-being of the city's inhabitants in mind.

Data Encryption and Confidentiality

Think of data encryption as constructing secure vaults within the Cloud City. Encrypting data ensures that even if unauthorized entities gain access, the information remains indecipherable. This human-centric approach safeguards sensitive information, respecting user privacy and instilling confidence in the security of cloud services.

Access Controls and Identity Management

Imagine access controls as the city's gates, and identity management as the system verifying who gets to enter. Cloud security involves implementing robust access controls and identity management protocols. This ensures that only authorized individuals can access specific data and services, preventing unauthorized entry and potential breaches.

Regular Audits and Compliance

Think of regular audits and compliance as city inspections to ensure structures meet safety standards. Cloud providers undergo regular audits to assess their security measures and ensure compliance with industry standards and regulations. This transparency fosters trust among users, assuring them that the Cloud City adheres to established security practices.

Navigating Human Elements: User Education and Collaboration

In the Cloud City, the principles of user education and collaboration are crucial. Just as citizens in a city collaborate for common goals, digital citizens must navigate through the Cloud City with a sense of awareness and shared responsibility.

User Education on Cloud Security

Consider user education on cloud security as providing a city guide to inhabitants. Cloud users need to be informed about best practices for securing their data, recognizing phishing attempts, and understanding the implications of shared responsibility. Education empowers users to make informed decisions in the cloud.

Collaborative Incident Response

Imagine collaborative incident response as emergency services working together during a crisis. In the event of a security incident, collaboration between cloud providers and users is essential. This involves timely communication, joint investigations, and coordinated efforts to mitigate the impact and prevent future incidents.

Real-world Application: Securing E- commerce Transactions in the Cloud City

Imagine a scenario where an e-commerce platform operates within the Cloud City, handling sensitive customer information and financial transactions. A secure approach unfolds as follows:

Secure Payment Processing

The e-commerce platform employs robust encryption protocols to secure payment transactions. This ensures that customers' financial data is protected during the entire transaction process, instilling trust in the security of online purchases.

Identity Verification

Access controls and identity management play a crucial role in verifying the identities of users and preventing unauthorized access to customer accounts. Multi-factor authentication is implemented to add an extra layer of security, ensuring that only authorized individuals can access sensitive information.

Regular Security Audits

The e-commerce platform undergoes regular security audits to assess vulnerabilities and compliance with Payment Card Industry Data Security Standard (PCI DSS) requirements. This proactive approach not only addresses potential risks but also demonstrates a commitment to maintaining a secure environment for customer transactions.

User Education on Account Security

The e-commerce platform conducts user education campaigns to inform customers about account security best practices. This includes guidance on creating strong passwords, recognizing phishing attempts, and utilizing security features such as two-factor authentication. Educated users become active participants in maintaining the security of their accounts.

INTERNET OF THINGS (IOT) SECURITY

In the interconnected landscape of digital technology, where everyday objects become intelligent nodes in the vast web of the Internet of Things (IoT), security stands as the guardian of this dynamic ecosystem. Picture the IoT as a city where devices communicate seamlessly, from smart thermostats and wearable's to industrial sensors. In this exploration, we navigate the human-centric dimensions of IoT security, threading the delicate balance between the convenience of interconnected devices and the imperative to fortify against potential risks.

Setting the Stage: The IoT City and Its Inhabitants

Imagine the IoT as a bustling city where devices exchange information, optimizing processes and enhancing daily life. In this city, IoT security becomes the gatekeeper, ensuring that the data flowing through these interconnected devices remains confidential, the devices themselves are not compromised, and the privacy of citizens is respected. Understanding this landscape begins with acknowledging the complexities of the IoT city.

Defining IoT Security

Consider defining IoT security as the measures put in place to protect the integrity, confidentiality, and availability of data transmitted between IoT devices and to safeguard the devices themselves from potential cyber threats. In the same way a city employs surveillance and safeguards for its residents, IoT security ensures the well-being of the connected ecosystem.

Navigating the Interconnected Web

Imagine navigating the interconnected web as understanding the intricate pathways through which devices communicate. Each device in the IoT city is like a citizen contributing to the collective intelligence. Navigating this web involves securing the communication channels to prevent unauthorized access and potential cyberattacks.

Crafting a Secure Ecosystem: A Human- Centric Perspective

In the face of technological advancements and the proliferation of IoT devices, crafting a secure ecosystem involves recognizing the impact of individual and collective actions on data privacy, user trust, and the overall stability of the IoT city. It's akin to urban planning, where architects design structures with the safety and well-being of the city's inhabitants in mind.

Ensuring Data Privacy

Think of ensuring data privacy as constructing private spaces within the IoT city. With a myriad of devices collecting and transmitting data, privacy becomes a paramount concern. IoT security involves implementing robust encryption measures to protect sensitive information, ensuring that citizens' data remains confidential.

Securing Device Identities

Imagine securing device identities as issuing digital IDs to citizens. Each IoT device needs a unique identity to participate in the city's activities. Security measures include the use of secure authentication protocols and the establishment of a trusted identity framework to prevent unauthorized devices from joining the ecosystem.

Monitoring for Anomalies

Think of monitoring for anomalies as having vigilant security personnel in the city. IoT security involves continuous monitoring of device behavior to detect unusual patterns or suspicious activities. Anomalies could indicate potential cyber threats, and early detection is essential to respond promptly and mitigate risks.

Navigating Human Elements: User Education and Collaboration

In the IoT city, the principles of user education and collaboration are crucial. Just as citizens in a city collaborate for common goals, digital citizens must navigate through the IoT city with a sense of awareness and shared responsibility.

User Education on IoT Security

Consider user education on IoT security as providing a guide to citizens on how to safely navigate the city. Users need to be informed about the risks associated with IoT devices, including potential privacy concerns and security best practices. Education empowers users to make informed decisions about the devices they integrate into their lives.

Collaborative Incident Response

Imagine collaborative incident response as emergency services working together during a crisis. In the event of a security incident, collaboration between IoT device manufacturers, service providers, and users is essential. This involves timely communication, joint investigations, and coordinated efforts to mitigate the impact and prevent future incidents.

Real-world Application: Securing Smart Home Devices in the IoT City

Imagine a scenario where a family relies on various smart home devices, from thermostats to security cameras, within the IoT city. A secure approach unfolds as follows:

Secure Device Configurations

The family ensures that each smart home device is configured securely, with strong passwords and updated firmware. This is akin to securing individual homes within the city to prevent unauthorized access.

Network Segmentation

The family employs network segmentation to create distinct zones for their IoT devices, separating them from critical systems. This is similar to zoning regulations in a city, ensuring that potential security breaches in one area do not compromise the entire network.

Regular Software Updates

The family stays vigilant about software updates for their smart home devices. Regular updates, like infrastructure maintenance in a city, ensure that security vulnerabilities are patched, reducing the risk of cyber threats.

User Education

The family educates all members about the potential risks and benefits of smart home devices. They emphasize the importance of privacy settings, responsible device use, and recognizing signs of suspicious activity. Education becomes a collective effort to ensure the security of their interconnected living space.

Chapter 12

FURTHER CONSIDERATIONS FOR RISK MANAGEMENT

Risk management is the ongoing process of identifying, assessing, prioritizing, and addressing risks to minimize their potential negative impact and maximize opportunities. It is a proactive and strategic approach to dealing with uncertainties, aimed at reducing the likelihood of adverse events and minimizing the potential consequences if they do occur. Risk management involves not only addressing known risks but also anticipating and preparing for potential future risks. It requires a combination of knowledge, skills, methodologies, and tools to effectively navigate the complex landscape of risks and make informed decisions.

The field of risk assessment and risk management is multidisciplinary, drawing from various disciplines such as finance, economics, engineering, psychology, and environmental sciences. It encompasses a wide range of activities, including risk identification, risk analysis, risk evaluation, risk treatment, risk communication, and risk monitoring. Depending on the nature of the risks and the context in which they occur, different techniques and approaches may be employed, such as qualitative assessments, quantitative modeling, scenario analysis, and decision trees.

Effective risk management and risk assessment have numerous benefits. They help organizations identify potential threats and opportunities, enhance decision-making processes, allocate resources effectively, improve project planning, and enhance overall performance and resilience. Risk management also enables organizations to comply with regulatory requirements, maintain stakeholder confidence, and adapt to changing business environments.

As risk management is a continuous process, it requires a proactive and systematic approach. It involves establishing a risk management framework, defining risk appetite and tolerance levels, implementing risk management strategies, regularly monitoring and reviewing risks, and adjusting mitigation plans as necessary. It also requires effective communication and collaboration among stakeholders to ensure a shared understanding of risks and facilitate informed decision-making.

Risk assessment and risk management are essential disciplines that enable individuals and organizations to navigate uncertainties and make informed decisions in a dynamic world. By identifying, analyzing, and mitigating risks, organizations can protect their assets, enhance their performance, and seize opportunities for growth and innovation. The study and practice of risk assessment and risk management provide valuable skills and knowledge that can be applied across industries and sectors, making it an indispensable field in today's rapidly evolving landscape.

In the field of risk management, it is critical to recognize that not all risks are necessarily bad or destructive to a company. While risks are frequently connected with potential harm, they can also bring chances for growth, innovation, and competitive advantage. Understanding the concept of risk appetite and creating a healthy risk culture are critical components in efficiently navigating the risk environment and maximizing the potential benefits.

Risk appetite refers to the level of risk that an organization is ready to accept or tolerate in order to achieve its goals. It reflects the organization's strategic goals, values, and the level of risk it is willing to accept to attain its intended outcomes. Risk appetite guides decision-makers by setting risk-taking boundaries and thresholds, guaranteeing a balanced approach that avoids extreme risk aversion or reckless behavior.

Organizations that have a clear and well-defined risk appetite can make informed judgments about prospective possibilities and dangers. Organizations can align their risk management activities with their strategic objectives and avoid unnecessary exposure or missed opportunities by developing an acceptable risk appetite. It also allows for effective communication and awareness of risk tolerance within the organization, helping workers to make risk-informed decisions within the scope of their jobs and responsibilities.

Risk culture refers to an organization's risk-related attitudes, values, beliefs, and practices. It embodies the collective risk-management philosophy and strategy that pervades the whole firm, from top-level executives to front-line personnel. A strong risk culture produces an atmosphere in which risk is viewed as an inherent aspect of decision- making and individuals are empowered to detect, assess, and manage risks effectively.

A positive risk culture promotes open communication, transparency, and accountability when it comes to risks. It fosters a proactive mindset in which risks are addressed, evaluated, and integrated into the organization's strategic planning processes.

A strong risk culture also promotes a continual learning and improvement mindset, in which lessons from previous events are shared and implemented to improve future risk management processes.

Notably, risk culture should relate to the organization's principles and integrated into its entire corporate culture. It should be backed by suitable policies, processes, and governance structures that promote risk awareness and prudent risk-taking at all levels of the company.

THE SYNERGY OF RISK APPETITE AND RISK CULTURE

Both risk appetite and risk culture are interrelated and mutually reinforcing. The values, attitudes, and behaviors of individuals inside an organization determine the organization's overall risk tolerance and appetite. In contrast, an organization's risk appetite helps shape its risk culture by providing a framework and rules for risk management procedures and decision-making processes.

Organizations may efficiently capitalize on opportunities while managing potential risks when their risk appetite and risk culture are matched and well-integrated. They foster a climate in which risk is viewed as a benefit rather than a burden to doing business. This proactive approach enables firms to recognize new risks, react to changing situations, and make educated decisions to enhance value generation while limiting potential negative repercussions.

Finally, knowing the ideas of risk appetite and risk culture, as well as recognizing that not all risks are bad, are critical for effective risk management. Organizations may grab opportunities, promote innovation, and succeed in an uncertain and ever-changing business environment by having a defined risk appetite and building a positive risk culture

DECISION MAKING

Making decisions is an essential part of our everyday life, both individually and professionally. Every day, we are presented with a plethora of options that need us to weigh various alternatives, analyze prospective outcomes, and finally decide. A methodical approach to decision-making that incorporates available information evaluates risks and benefits, and corresponds with our aims and beliefs is required for effective decision-making. In this note, we will look at the decision-making process and present specific examples to demonstrate various decision-making strategies and scenarios.

Rational Decision-Making

Rational decision-making is a methodical process that entails obtaining relevant information, recognizing alternatives, weighing their advantages and disadvantages, and picking the optimal option. This method is frequently utilized in business and organizational contexts. As an example: Consider yourself a project manager in charge of picking a software development vendor for a key project. You would conduct research, gather proposals from various vendors, evaluate their capabilities, consider factors such as cost, quality, and expertise, and finally select the vendor that best aligns with the project requirements and organizational goals.

Making Intuitive Decisions

Without a rigorous study, intuitive decision-making depends on instinct, gut feelings, and past experiences to make choices. This method is useful when time is limited or the decision is based on subjective criteria. As an example: When negotiating a transaction with a client, as an experienced salesperson, you may rely on your intuition. You may make quick decisions regarding pricing, product positioning, and concessions based on your gut feelings and a sense of what has worked in comparable situations, drawing on your expertise and knowledge of the market.

Making Decisions Together

Collaborative decision-making entails involving numerous stakeholders and soliciting their thoughts and opinions in order to reach an agreement. This method is useful when multiple perspectives and skills are necessary to make an informed conclusion. Consider the following scenario: Team members may engage in collaborative decision-making in a team-based project by conducting regular meetings, brainstorming ideas, discussing various choices, and collectively agreeing on the best course of action. Each team member provides their own unique perspective, and they work together to reach a consensus that benefits the entire team.

Making Ethical Decisions

Ethical decision-making entails considering moral principles, values, and ethical standards while making decisions. This method ensures that judgments are ethical and have a good influence on individuals and society. Here is an illustration: The management team of a corporation is faced with the decision to lay off many people in order to save money. Ethical decision-making would include considering the influence on employees, their families, and the larger community. Decision-makers would assess the financial necessity against the ethical responsibility to treat employees fairly, to provide support, and explore options to mitigate the negative impact.

Making Risk-Based Decisions

Assessing the risks and uncertainties associated with several options and selecting the one with the best risk-reward tradeoff is what risk-based decision-making entails. This method is frequently employed in financial and project management contexts. Consider the following scenario: An investor is weighing the pros and cons of two investment opportunities: one with possibly larger returns but higher risks, and one with lower profits but reduced dangers. To make an informed decision that balances risk and return based on their risk appetite and investment objectives, the investor would undertake a risk assessment, examining factors such as market volatility, industry trends, and regulatory changes.

Making good decisions is an important ability to have in both personal and professional situations. Individuals and organizations can negotiate difficult situations, manage risks, and achieve their goals by understanding and employing diverse decision-making approaches such as logical, intuitive, collaborative, ethical, and risk-based decision- making. Consider the examples offered to get insight into the practical implementation of these decision-making techniques.

Chapter 13

RISK IDENTIFICATION AND ASSESSMENT

Identification of risks is the essential first stage in risk management. It involves meticulously identifying and documenting potential risks that could have an impact on the accomplishment of organizational objectives or project outcomes. By proactively identifying risks, organizations can develop strategies to mitigate or exploit them, thereby improving their capacity to respond effectively to unanticipated events.

During the risk identification phase, it is crucial to involve stakeholders from a variety of organizational levels in order to collect diverse perspectives and ensure comprehensive coverage of potential risks. This inclusive approach facilitates a more in-depth comprehension of the organization's operations, processes, and external environment, allowing for a more comprehensive risk assessment.

There are numerous techniques and methods available for identifying hazards. Here are some prevalent approaches:

Brainstorming

This method entails assembling a group of individuals with diverse expertise and knowledge in order to generate a list of potential dangers. The participants communicate their ideas freely, fostering creative thought and revealing risks that may not have been initially apparent.

Documentation Evaluation

By evaluating organizational documents such as policies, procedures, project plans, and historical data, valuable insights into past incidents, issues, or obstacles can be gained. This analysis aids in the identification of recurrent risks or those associated with activities or processes.

Surveys and Interviews

Interviewing or surveying key stakeholders can provide valuable insight into their experiences, concerns, and risk perceptions. This method assists in identifying risks that may not be immediately apparent and provides a qualitative comprehension of the impact and probability of identified risks.

Checklists

Using predefined protocols or risk registers can facilitate the systematic identification of risks based on industry standards, regulations, or past experiences. Checklists serve as a guide to guarantee that common hazards are not missed during the identification process.

SWOT Analysis

SWOT Analysis is a powerful strategic planning tool used to evaluate the strengths, weaknesses, opportunities, and threats of an individual, organization, or project. By conducting a SWOT

Analysis, one can gain valuable insights into the internal and external factors that can influence their objectives and decision-making processes. This note will provide a detailed explanation of each component of the SWOT Analysis, along with illustrative examples.

Strengths

Strengths refer to the internal positive attributes or capabilities that give an individual, organization, or project a competitive advantage. These are factors that contribute to success and differentiation. Examples of strengths may include:
- Strong brand reputation and recognition.
- Skilled and experienced workforce.
- High-quality products or services.
- Robust financial position.
- Efficient supply chain management.
- Effective internal communication and teamwork.

Weaknesses

Weaknesses are internal factors that hinder an individual, organization, or project from achieving optimal performance or competitive advantage. Identifying weaknesses allows for targeted improvement efforts. Examples of weaknesses may include:
- The limited market presence or brand awareness.
- Lack of technological infrastructure.
- Inadequate financial resources.
- Inefficient operational processes.
- Skill gaps or insufficient training.
- Poor customer service.

Opportunities

Opportunities are external factors that present favorable circumstances for growth, expansion, or improvement. Identifying opportunities enables individuals or organizations to capitalize on emerging trends or market conditions. Examples of opportunities may include:

- New market segments or untapped customer demographics.
- Technological advancements can improve efficiency.
- Changes in government regulations or policies.
- Collaborative partnerships or strategic alliances.
- Growing demand for a particular product or service.
- Economic or market trends that align with existing capabilities.

Threats

Threats are external factors that pose challenges or risks to an individual, organization, or project's success. Identifying threats allows for proactive planning and risk mitigation strategies. Examples of threats may include:

- Intense competition within the industry.
- Economic downturns or market volatility.
- Rapid technological advancements render current offerings obsolete.
- Changing consumer preferences or buying behavior.
- Legal or regulatory challenges.
- Supplier or vendor reliability issues.

It is important to note that strengths and weaknesses are internal to the individual or organization, while opportunities and threats are external factors in the broader environment. The goal of conducting a SWOT Analysis is to leverage strengths, address weaknesses, capitalize on opportunities, and mitigate threats to develop effective strategies and make informed decisions.

By considering the combination of internal strengths and weaknesses with external opportunities and threats, individuals and organizations can develop actionable plans that align with their objectives and maximize their chances of success.

SWOT Analysis provides a comprehensive framework for assessing the current state and future prospects of an individual, organization, or project. It helps identify key areas for improvement, potential growth avenues, and risks to be managed. Through a thoughtful and thorough SWOT Analysis, individuals and organizations can gain valuable insights that inform their strategic decision-making processes.

Scenario Analysis

Processes to explore various potential future outcomes and their associated risks and opportunities. It involves the creation of multiple plausible scenarios or narratives to evaluate the potential impact of different factors and events on a given situation or project. By considering a range of scenarios, organizations can enhance their preparedness, identify potential vulnerabilities, and develop effective strategies to navigate uncertain environments.

Here are some examples of Scenario Analysis:

Financial Sector

Imagine a scenario where a global recession occurs due to a major financial crisis. In this scenario, interest rates rise, stock markets crash, and credit becomes tight. Financial institutions face increased default risks, liquidity challenges, and regulatory pressures. By conducting scenario analysis, banks and investment firms can assess their vulnerability to such a situation and develop contingency plans to ensure their financial stability, such as diversifying their investment portfolios, stress-testing their balance sheets, and strengthening risk management practices.

Energy Industry

Consider a scenario where there is a significant disruption in the global oil supply due to political tensions or natural disasters. This scenario leads to a sudden increase in oil prices, causing economic shocks and impacting industries heavily reliant on petroleum products. Energy companies can use scenario analysis to evaluate the potential consequences of such an event, explore alternative energy sources, invest in renewable energy technologies, and diversify their operations to reduce dependence on fossil fuels.

Technology Start-up

Suppose a technology start-up is developing a new product and faces uncertainties regarding market adoption, competition, and regulatory changes. By conducting scenario analysis, the start-up can create multiple scenarios that explore different market conditions, customer preferences, and competitive landscapes. This analysis helps the start-up identify potential risks, anticipate market shifts, and adjust its business strategy accordingly. For example, scenario analysis might reveal the need for additional investments in research and development, adjusting the product pricing, or exploring new markets.

Supply Chain Management

Imagine a scenario where a global pandemic disrupts supply chains, causing shortages of critical components and raw materials. Manufacturers heavily reliant on international suppliers' experience production delays, increased costs, and customer dissatisfaction. By conducting scenario analysis, companies can identify vulnerabilities in their supply chains, explore alternative sourcing options, establish strategic stockpiles, or develop contingency plans to ensure business continuity in the face of supply chain disruptions.

Environmental Impact

Consider a scenario where stricter environmental regulations are implemented, requiring companies to reduce their carbon emissions and adopt sustainable practices. Through scenario analysis, organizations can explore different regulatory frameworks, carbon pricing mechanisms, and market demands for environmentally friendly products. This analysis helps companies anticipate and adapt to future environmental requirements, such as investing in renewable energy, optimizing production processes, or developing eco- friendly products to gain a competitive edge.

In each of these examples, scenario analysis enables organizations to assess the potential impact of various factors, make informed decisions, and develop strategies that enhance resilience and adaptability. By considering multiple scenarios, organizations can proactively manage risks, seize opportunities, and position themselves for success in an uncertain and dynamic business environment.

Throughout the process of risk identification, it is essential to note identified risks in a structured manner, capturing pertinent details such as risk descriptions, potential causes, potential consequences, and their associated sources. This information serves as the foundation for subsequent risk evaluation and analysis.

Risk identification is an ongoing process that should be revisited frequently to account for new threats that may arise as a result of changing conditions. It is crucial to cultivate a risk-aware culture within the organization, urging all stakeholders to remain vigilant and report potential risks as they arise.

Identification of risks is the first stage in effective risk management. By employing a variety of techniques and involving stakeholders, organizations can comprehensively and proactively identify potential risks. This procedure lays the groundwork for subsequent risk evaluation, analysis, and the development of appropriate risk response strategies.

RISK ASSESSMENT

In the realm of risk management, risk assessment is a crucial procedure involving the identification, evaluation, and prioritization of potential risks to determine their likelihood and potential impact. It serves as the foundation for effective risk management strategies, allowing individuals and organizations to make informed decisions and allocate resources to mitigate or address risks appropriately.

The primary objective of risk assessment is to analyze and quantify risks systematically in order to comprehend their nature, severity, and potential consequences. This procedure includes a few essential stages that aid in identifying and comprehending risks comprehensively.

Identifying and recognizing the potential hazards an organization or project may face is the initial step in risk assessment. This requires a comprehensive analysis of internal and external factors, such as processes, systems, stakeholders, industry trends, and regulatory requirements. Techniques for identifying risks, such as ideation, checklists, and historical data analysis, are frequently used to identify a wide variety of risks.

Risk analysis is an important part of the risk management process since it involves identifying and evaluating potential hazards to determine their likelihood and impact. It assists organizations in risk prioritization and making informed decisions about risk treatment and mitigation measures. Depending on the complexity and availability of data, risk analysis can be done qualitatively or quantitatively. Let us take a closer look at risk analysis with some examples:

Qualitative Risk Analysis

This is a subjective assessment of hazards based on their features and impact. It does not rely on numerical data to assess hazards, instead employing descriptive scales. The following are some examples of qualitative risk analysis techniques.

- Risk Probability and Impact Assessment
In this technique, subjective probabilities and impact levels are assigned to detected risks. Based on their experience and knowledge, a project manager might grade the likelihood of a project delay as "high" and the impact as "moderate."

- Risk categorization
Risks are classified according to their nature or source, for example, financial risks, operational risks, technological

risks, or legal risks. Categorization aids in comprehending the many sorts of hazards and their possible impact on various elements of the company.

- Risk Scoring

Risk scoring entails assigning risk scores or ratings based on predetermined criteria. A risk matrix, for example, can be used to classify hazards as low, medium, or high depending on their likelihood and impact. This enables organizations to prioritize hazards for future investigation and mitigation.

Quantitative Risk Analysis

Quantitative risk analysis is a more objective, data-driven approach to risk assessment. It quantifies the likelihood and potential impact of hazards using numerical data and statistical methodologies. Among the quantitative risk analysis approaches are as follows.

- Monte Carlo Method

Monte Carlo simulation is the process of performing many simulations based on probabilistic inputs in order to examine the range of possible outcomes and their associated probabilities. It is frequently used in financial risk analysis to evaluate investment portfolios, pricing models, and project timelines.

- Sensitivity Analysis

The influence of modifying input factors on the overall outcome or outcomes is assessed using sensitivity analysis. It aids in identifying the most crucial variables that have a major impact on risk exposure. In a manufacturing process, for example, sensitivity analysis can quantify the impact of differences in raw material costs on project profitability.

- Expected Monetary Value (EMV) Analysis

The expected value of each risk event is calculated using EMV analysis by multiplying the likelihood of occurrence by the related impact or cost. It enables businesses to prioritize risks based on their potential financial impact and identify the most cost- effective risk mitigation methods.

As an example, consider a construction job. The project team evaluates potential hazards during the risk analysis phase, such as severe weather conditions, labor shortages, design revisions, and material price fluctuations. The team then uses qualitative or quantitative methodologies to analyze the likelihood and impact of each risk.

For qualitative analysis, the team might rank the possibility of poor weather conditions as "medium" and the impact as "high" because it can cause project delays and cost increases. Similarly, the team may rank labor shortages as "low" but having a "high" impact because they can reduce productivity and increase overtime expenses.

The team may utilize previous weather data to determine the risk of poor weather conditions and estimate the cost of delay for quantitative analysis. They may also examine past labor market trends to assess the possibility of labor shortages and the financial implications.

The project team can prioritize risks, build contingency plans, allocate resources, and make informed judgments on risk treatment tactics such as contractual agreements, schedule buffers, or alternate sourcing possibilities based on the risk analysis findings.

Remember that risk analysis provides useful insights into

prospective risks, helping organizations to better manage resources, prepare contingencies, and make proactive actions to reduce the impact of uncertainty.

Risk Evaluation

A key component of risk management is risk evaluation, which is evaluating and classifying hazards according to their importance and likelihood of occurring in order to assign them a priority. It seeks to give a thorough understanding of the hazards discovered during the risk assessment phase and empowers businesses to decide on effective risk management and mitigation techniques.

The following essential factors are considered while evaluating risks:

- Risk Severity: This term describes the possible effects or impact that a risk occurrence could have on the goals, operations, assets, or reputation of an organization. Normally, risks are rated on a qualitative or quantitative scale, considering things like monetary loss, safety risks, potential legal or regulatory repercussions, operational interruptions, and reputational harm.

- Risk Likelihood: This term describes the likelihood or regularity of a risk event happening. To calculate the possibility of risks, historical data, expert opinions, statistical models, or other pertinent sources of information are analyzed. A qualitative or quantitative scale, ranging from low to high or from rare to regular, is typically used to rate likelihood.

- Risk Tolerance: The ability of a stakeholder or organization to accept or tolerate a particular level of risk. It demonstrates the organization's tolerance for risk and establishes the acceptable degree of exposure to various dangers. The organization's aims, sector, legal constraints, and other contextual elements may all influence risk tolerance.

- Risk Prioritization: After hazards are ranked according to their likelihood and seriousness, they are prioritized to determine how best to deal with them. The highest priority risks are often those with a high probability of occurrence and necessitate quick attention and mitigation strategies. Prioritization aids in efficient resource allocation and concentrates attention on the most important risks that carry the greatest potential for harm or impact.

- Risk Assessment Methodologies: Depending on the type of risk and the information at hand, many approaches can be used to undertake risk evaluation. Risks are given subjective values or scores using qualitative risk assessment techniques like risk matrices or risk scoring based on their significance and likelihood. On the other side, quantitative risk assessment techniques entail employing statistical models, simulations, or calculations to calculate the numerical probabilities and potential economic effects of hazards.

In general, risk evaluation offers a methodical and structured way to comprehending the significance of risks, enabling firms to effectively allocate resources, and put into place risk management procedures. By considering the possible outcomes and likelihood of risks, aligning them with the organization's risk tolerance and objectives, and assuring a proactive approach to risk management, it facilitates decision-making.

Risk Treatment

Risk treatment, also known as risk response, is an important element in risk management. It entails choosing and implementing methods to address identified risks and their potential consequences. Risk management seeks to reduce or eliminate risks, transfer, or share risks with other parties, accept risks within established tolerances, or avoid risks entirely. Risk treatment's goal is to lessen the frequency and severity of negative consequences linked with identified risks.

In risk management, four basic tactics are typically used:

- Risk Avoidance: This method entails taking purposeful steps to remove or prevent dangers. It could include avoiding some activities, stopping processes or projects, or rejecting chances that pose too many risks. Risk avoidance is commonly used when the possible negative consequences of a risk outweigh the benefits or when suitable alternatives are available.

- Risk Reduction or Mitigation: Risk reduction or mitigation is the proactive use of actions to reduce the chance or impact of identified risks. The goal of this technique is to regulate and reduce the occurrence and severity of risks. adopting safety measures, performing regular inspections and maintenance, improving security protocols, adopting redundancy measures, or adding controls and safeguards are all examples of risk mitigation tactics. The goal is to lower the likelihood of a risk event occurring or to reduce the effect of an event that does occur.

- Risk Transfer: Risk transfer entails transferring some or all the risks to another party, generally through contracts or insurance arrangements. Organizations or individuals can protect themselves from any financial or operational losses connected with a risk event by shifting the risk. Purchasing insurance policies, outsourcing tasks to other parties, or entering into agreements that assign responsibility for specific risks to other entities are all examples of risk transfer.

- Risk Acceptance: Risk acceptance is a method that involves deliberately acknowledging and enduring the potential consequences of risks without taking explicit steps to mitigate them. When the costs of risk treatment outweigh the possible benefits, or when the possibility or impact of a risk is assessed to be within tolerable bounds, this technique is often used. Accepting risks does not imply ignoring them, but rather making an informed decision to manage and monitor them within established parameters.

It is crucial to highlight that risk management strategies are not mutually exclusive, and a variety of strategies may be used based on the nature of the risks and organizational objectives. The selection of effective risk treatment solutions necessitates a thorough examination of the risks' possible consequences, available resources, risk appetite, and organizational restrictions.

Effective risk treatment requires continual monitoring and frequent review to ensure that the chosen solutions remain relevant and successful in the changing risk landscape. Organizations may increase their resilience, preserve their assets, and make educated decisions that balance risk and reward by employing appropriate risk management practices.

Risk Monitoring and Evaluation

Risk assessment is a continuous process requiring ongoing surveillance and evaluation. Risks are dynamic and subject to change over time as a result of factors such as market conditions, technological advances, and regulatory modifications. Regular monitoring and review aid in the identification of new risks, the evaluation of the efficacy of implemented risk remedies, and the adjustment of risk management strategies as necessary. By remaining proactive and vigilant, organizations can maintain a robust risk management framework and adapt to emergent risks.

Effective risk assessment necessitates a multidisciplinary approach incorporating collaboration between diverse stakeholders, such as risk managers, subject matter experts, project managers, and senior management. It makes well-informed decisions based on accurate and trustworthy data, informed analysis, and sound judgment.

By conducting comprehensive risk assessments, organizations can anticipate potential threats and opportunities, manage uncertainties proactively, and improve their ability to achieve goals while minimizing the negative impact of risks. In strategic planning, project management, compliance, and overall business resiliency, risk assessment is a crucial tool.

Risk assessment is a fundamental risk management process that allows individuals and organizations to comprehend, evaluate, and rank risks. It enables the development of effective risk mitigation strategies and the making of informed decisions. By adopting a systematic and structured risk assessment methodology, organizations can confidently navigate uncertainty and nurture a culture of resilience and adaptability.

Here are a few examples to illustrate risk monitoring and evaluation in different contexts:

- Project Risk Monitoring and Evaluation

Risk monitoring in a construction project entails regularly tracking and assessing numerous project risks, such as material delivery delays, unfavorable weather conditions, or contractor performance concerns. A risk register can be used by project managers to record and monitor risks throughout the project's lifecycle. They can discover prospective risks that have formed or evolved through monitoring, update risk likelihood and impact estimates, and take the appropriate actions to successfully reduce or respond to the risks.

- Financial Risk Monitoring and Evaluation

To preserve stability and compliance, financial institutions regularly monitor and evaluate financial risks. A bank, for example, may monitor the credit risks connected with its lending portfolio. They review borrowers' creditworthiness on a regular basis, watch changes in economic conditions, and analyze the probable impact on loan defaults. Banks might change their lending procedures, create risk mitigation methods, or designate additional provisions for probable losses by monitoring these risks.

- Operational Risk Monitoring and Evaluation

To maintain smooth and effective operations, a manufacturing organization may monitor and evaluate operational risks.

This could entail keeping an eye out for risks such as equipment failure, supply chain interruptions, or process inefficiencies. Regular reviews allow the organization to discover areas for improvement, adopt preventive maintenance measures, and improve process controls in order to eliminate potential risks and optimize operational performance.

• Information Security Risk Monitoring and Evaluation
Organizations monitor and analyze risks in the field of information security in order to safeguard their data and systems against cyber threats. This includes monitoring network traffic in real-time, conducting vulnerability assessments, and reviewing security incident reports. Organizations can use evaluation to identify potential security flaws, assess the effectiveness of existing security measures, and take proactive steps to address vulnerabilities, such as implementing stronger access controls, updating software patches, or providing employee cybersecurity best practices training.

Chapter 14

RISK PRIORITIZATION AND MITIGATION

RISK PRIORITIZATION

Risk prioritization is an important part of good risk management since it guides decision- making processes. Organizations face multiple risks in today's complex and uncertain business environment, and it is critical to deploy resources efficiently to handle the most significant threats and opportunities.

Risk prioritization entails assessing and rating risks based on their possible impact and likelihood, allowing companies to focus their resources on the most important issues. Organizations can allocate resources, establish appropriate risk response plans, and adopt mitigation measures to lower the chance and effect of bad events by prioritizing risks.

There are many factors that influence risk prioritization, including,

Impact

A fundamental consideration in risk prioritization is the potential impact or repercussions of a risk. Risks that have the potential to cause considerable injury, financial loss, or disruption to vital activities are usually prioritized. The financial, reputational, environmental, and operational effects can all be measured. Let us consider a manufacturing company that is significantly reliant on a single source for a vital raw material utilized in their manufacturing process. The company recognizes a danger relating to the supplier's financial stability. If the supplier went bankrupt or experienced substantial financial difficulties, there would be a shortage of the raw material, disrupting production and perhaps inflicting significant financial losses for the company.

In terms of impact, the repercussions of this risk can include:

- Financial Loss: As a result of the production standstill and inability to fulfill customer orders, the company may suffer significant financial losses. This could include missed revenue, contract breach fines, and additional costs involved with finding a replacement supplier or reducing the impact.

- Reputational Damage: Failure to meet client requests owing to raw material shortages may result in discontent, unfavorable reviews, and reputational harm. This can result in the loss of existing clients as well as difficulty recruiting new ones.

- Operational Disruption: A supply chain disruption can have a domino impact on the company's operations. Inefficiencies, delays, and challenges in meeting production schedules may result, potentially harming other suppliers, employees, and overall corporate performance.

- Market Share Loss: Prolonged production disruptions can allow competitors to grab market share that the company is unable to supply. This can have long-term consequences for the company's market position and revenue.

The impact of this risk would be rated severe given the probable severity of these consequences. As a result, the risk is likely to be prioritized for immediate attention and risk mitigation steps such as preparing contingency plans, diversifying suppliers, or establishing alternate sourcing possibilities.

Organizations may effectively allocate resources and focus on resolving the risks that have the greatest potential to cause severe harm or disruption by evaluating the impact of risks. This strategy provides proactive risk management and contributes to the organization's resilience and sustainability.

Likelihood

Another important consideration in risk prioritizing is the possibility or probability of a risk occurring. Risks that are more likely to occur are frequently prioritized more promptly because they provide a bigger immediate threat. Historical data, expert judgment, statistical analysis, or predictive algorithms can all be used to determine probability.

Assume you are a risk manager for a company that manufactures electronic equipment. One of the risks you are evaluating is the possibility of a supply chain disruption caused by a natural disaster. You evaluate historical data, expert opinions, and current environmental conditions to determine the likelihood. You discover that the region in which your key suppliers are located is prone to earthquakes and has previously undergone numerous large seismic disasters.

Based on this information, you anticipate that an earthquake will cause a moderate to high supply chain disruption during the next five years. This disruption could result in production delays, revenue loss, and reputational harm.

You rate this risk as high due to the enormous impact such a disruption could have on your firm. You devote resources to developing contingency plans, such as finding alternative suppliers, creating supply chain redundancy, and enhancing communication links with suppliers, in order to assist speedy recovery in the case of an earthquake.

The chance of a supply chain disruption caused by an earthquake affects risk prioritization in this example. Risk management prioritizes this risk over others due to the potential impact of the risk and the moderate to high frequency of occurrence. By focusing resources on minimizing this risk, the business is better equipped to respond to and mitigate the effects of a potential supply chain disruption.

It is crucial to highlight that likelihood estimates are subjective and should be based on the most up-to-date facts and knowledge available. Changes in the environment, technology, or industry factors that may influence the risk landscape should be reviewed and reassessed on a regular basis.

Vulnerability

An important consideration is an organization's or system's vulnerability to a certain risk. Risks that exploit existing vulnerabilities or flaws in controls and safeguards may be prioritized higher because they are more likely to cause harm. Understanding the organization's infrastructure, operations, and security measures is required for assessing vulnerabilities.

Consider a multinational organization that relies significantly on its IT infrastructure to hold sensitive customer data, manage financial transactions, and support vital business activities. In this scenario, the vulnerability could be characterized as a lack of adequate cybersecurity protections within the organization's network.

Factors that may lead to this vulnerability include:

- Outdated Software: The Company may be employing obsolete software or operating systems that are no longer receiving security updates or fixes. This exposes the network to known exploits and malware assaults.

- Weak Password Policies: The organization's password regulations may be lax, allowing employees to use passwords that are easily guessable or regularly used. This raises the possibility of unauthorized access to critical data and systems.

- Insufficient Employee Training: Employees may not receive proper cybersecurity best practices training, such as recognizing phishing emails, avoiding dubious websites, or securely handling sensitive information. This lack of awareness raises the possibility of human error resulting in security breaches.

- Inadequate Firewall and Intrusion Detection Systems: The organization's firewalls and intrusion detection systems may be obsolete or inadequately configured, making it simpler for hackers to obtain unauthorized access to the network or exploit system vulnerabilities.

- Lack of Regular Security Assessments: The organization may not perform regular security assessments or penetration testing to uncover vulnerabilities and flaws in its network architecture. Because of this lack of proactive assessment, potential vulnerabilities are undiscovered and neglected.

- Third-Party Dependencies: The firm may rely extensively on third-party vendors or suppliers for a variety of IT services, such as cloud storage or software solutions. If these suppliers' security efforts are poor, it presents new vulnerabilities that can be exploited.

The presence of these vulnerabilities raises the organization's vulnerability to cyber threats such as data breaches, ransomware attacks, and unauthorized access to critical information. As a result, prioritizing vulnerability mitigation becomes critical in the risk management process. The organization may invest resources to address each vulnerability, such as adopting software updates, enforcing strong password regulations, conducting employee training programs, improving network security measures, and monitoring the efficiency of their cybersecurity safeguards on a regular basis.

Organizations may enhance their defenses, minimize the risk and effect of possible cyber assaults, and secure their vital assets and operations by detecting and fixing vulnerabilities.

Strategic Alignment

Prioritization should be in line with the strategic aims and objectives of the firm. Risks that have a direct influence on achieving strategic objectives or are directly related to important business processes should be prioritized. This guarantees that risk management efforts are directed at safeguarding the organization's critical interests and priorities.

Consider the imaginary XYZ Corporation, which operates in the technology business. Several strategic goals have been defined by the corporation, including increasing market share, expanding into new areas, and improving customer happiness. XYZ Corporation considers the following scenario to link risk priority with these strategic goals:

- Market Share: Increasing XYZ Corporation's market share is one of its strategic aims. Risks that could directly affect market share, such as severe competition, disruptive technologies, or poor customer reviews, would be given higher importance in risk prioritization. XYZ Corporation guarantees that its efforts are aimed on safeguarding and improving its market position by focusing on these risks.

- New Market Expansion: Expansion into new markets is another strategic goal. To ensure a seamless and effective expansion, risks connected with market entry, such as regulatory compliance, cultural diversity, or geopolitical instability, would be prioritized. By proactively addressing these risks, XYZ Corporation may reduce potential roadblocks and increase its chances of effectively entering new markets.

- Customer Satisfaction: XYZ Corporation places a high value on customer satisfaction. Risks that potentially have an influence on consumer satisfaction, such as product quality issues, service disruptions, or data breaches, would be prioritized higher. By focusing on these risks, the company hopes to safeguard its reputation, keep customers loyal, and ultimately achieve its strategic goal of increasing customer satisfaction.

In this instance, XYZ Corporation's risk prioritizing is aligned with its strategic goals. The organization ensures that its risk management efforts are directed toward defending its strategic interests by identifying and prioritizing risks that have a direct influence on market share, new market expansion, and customer satisfaction. This strategic alignment enables XYZ Corporation to effectively manage resources and make informed decisions to mitigate the most essential risks while supporting its long-term business objectives.

It should be noted that the specific strategic alignment criteria and priorities may differ based on the business, industry, and market conditions. Each organization's risk prioritization strategy should be tailored to its own strategic goals and objectives.

Regulatory and Legal Requirements

Compliance with regulatory and legal requirements is an important factor to consider when prioritizing risks. To ensure compliance with applicable rules and regulations, risks that could result in noncompliance, legal obligations, or regulatory punishments are often prioritized. This is especially true in areas with strict regulatory frameworks, such as finance, healthcare, and energy.

Here are some examples of regulatory requirements:

- Anti-Money Laundering (AML) Regulations: To avoid money laundering and terrorist financing, financial institutions must apply stringent AML measures. This includes performing customer due diligence, monitoring transactions, and reporting questionable activity to regulatory authorities.

- Know Your Customer (KYC) Requirements: To reduce

the risk of fraud, identity theft, and financial crimes, financial institutions must verify and document the identification of their customers. KYC procedures entail gathering data such as identification documents, proof of address, and beneficial ownership information.

- Data Protection and Privacy Laws: To maintain the confidentiality and security of client information, financial institutions must follow data protection and privacy laws. Obtaining consent for data gathering, establishing proper safeguards, and giving persons control over their personal data are all part of this.

- Securities Regulations: Securities regulations govern the issuance, trading, and disclosure of financial market securities. These rules are intended to safeguard investors, ensure fair and transparent markets, and prohibit fraudulent activity. Registration, reporting, and disclosure obligations are all part of complying with securities legislation.

- Consumer Protection Laws: To protect the interests of clients, financial institutions are subject to consumer protection legislation. These regulations govern activities such as fair lending, term and cost information, and the processing of consumer complaints. Consumer protection laws assist to ensure equitable treatment of customers and the prevention of abusive behavior.

- Sarbanes-Oxley Act (SOX): The SOX Act governs financial reporting, internal controls, and corporate governance for publicly traded firms. It seeks to improve openness, accountability, and integrity in financial reporting in order to safeguard investors and restore public trust in financial markets.

- Payment Card Industry Data Security Standard (PCI DSS): PCI DSS is a set of security rules that govern payment card data protection. It applies to institutions such as banks, retailers, and payment processors that handle cardholder information. PCI DSS compliance aids in the prevention of payment card fraud and data breaches.

- Basel III is a global banking regulatory framework that establishes minimum capital requirements, liquidity norms, and risk management principles. By addressing vulnerabilities discovered during the 2008 financial crisis, it attempts to increase bank resilience and promote financial stability.

These are only a few instances of financial industry regulatory and legal requirements. Organizations in this sector must be knowledgeable about the unique legislation that apply to their area and ensure compliance to avoid legal ramifications, reputational loss, and financial penalties.

Stakeholder concerns

Stakeholder concerns and priorities might impact risk prioritization. Customers, employees, investors, regulatory organizations, and the general public are all examples of stakeholders. Risks that are of particular concern to stakeholders, such as those harming public safety or the environment, may be prioritized in order to retain stakeholder trust and confidence.

- Customers: Customers are an important stakeholder group for any business. Customer safety, product quality, data security, and privacy concerns can all have a substantial impact on risk prioritizing. To ensure customer happiness and loyalty, risks that have the potential to harm customers, undermine their trust or result in unsatisfied experiences may be prioritized.

- Employees: Organizations place a high value on employee well-being and safety. Workplace dangers, occupational health and safety, harassment, discrimination, or insufficient training can all have a negative influence on employee morale and productivity. To safeguard the workers and preserve a pleasant work environment, such risks may be prioritized.

- Investors: Investors and shareholders are worried about an organization's financial stability and profitability. Market instability, economic downturns, supply chain disruptions, and regulatory changes, for example, may be prioritized to protect investor interests and retain shareholder value.

- Regulatory Bodies: Organizations operating in regulated environments must comply with laws, regulations, and industry standards. Risks that could result in noncompliance, legal action, or penalties may be prioritized to ensure regulatory compliance and a strong relationship with regulatory agencies.

- Local Communities: Organizations that operate in specific geographical areas owe it to local communities to consider their concerns. To address community concerns and maintain a positive reputation in the local region, risks with possible repercussions on the environment, public health, or community well-being may be prioritized.

- Suppliers and Partners: Organizations rely on suppliers

and partners to keep their operations running smoothly. Supply chain disruptions, vendor dependability, and contractual commitments can all have an impact on an organization's capacity to deliver products or services. Prioritizing risks affecting the organization's core suppliers or key partners aids in ensuring continuity and minimizing disruptions.

- Public and Media: Public perception and media coverage can have a substantial impact on an organization's reputation and brand image. To safeguard the organization's image and retain public trust, risks that have the potential to draw unwanted attention, damage the brand's reputation, or provoke public uproar may be prioritized.

When prioritizing risks, firms must engage stakeholders proactively, understand their issues, and weigh their opinions. Organizations can develop trust, strengthen relationships, and improve their entire risk management strategy by addressing stakeholder concerns.

Available resources

The availability of resources, such as finance, manpower, and time, can also have an impact on risk prioritizing. Organizations must examine their ability to effectively handle and reduce risks. Risks that may be addressed with existing resources or through cost- effective solutions may be prioritized higher, but risks that need significant resources may be prioritized differently.

Consider a manufacturing corporation that wants to prioritize risks in their manufacturing process. In this situation, available resources could include:

- Budget: The Company's budget for risk management operations is restricted. Risks that may be addressed within the specified budget may be prioritized higher since they can be mitigated without exceeding budgetary restrictions. Risks requiring large financial expenditure, on the other hand, may be deprioritized or demand further explanation.

- Personnel: A risk management team is in place at the organization. Personnel availability and expertise can have an impact on risk prioritizing. Risks that are aligned with the team's abilities and experience can be addressed more effectively, but risks that require specialist knowledge or additional manpower may be prioritized lower or require external assistance.

- Time: Time is a valuable resource for dealing with dangers. Risks that constitute an immediate threat or have a greater potential impact in a short period of time may be prioritized for quick action. Dangers with longer-term repercussions or dangers that may be addressed over a longer timeframe, on the other hand, may be prioritized differently, considering the urgency of other risks.

- Technology and Infrastructure: The technological capabilities and infrastructure of the organization influence risk prioritization. Risks that may be handled using existing technology solutions or infrastructure may be prioritized since they can be executed with minimal effort. Risks that necessitate significant upgrades or infrastructure improvements may be reprioritized or necessitate a longer-term plan.

- External Support: The availability of external assistance, such as consultants or specialist service providers, might influence risk prioritizing. Risks that necessitate the use of outside expertise or resources may be prioritized based on the availability and cost- effectiveness of such assistance. The corporation may choose to devote resources to hazards that can be effectively addressed with outside help.

In this instance, the manufacturing organization must prioritize risks based on its available resources. They may choose to prioritize risks based on their budget, personnel capabilities, time restrictions, available technology, and infrastructure. By efficiently employing its current resources, the organization may focus on tackling the most significant issues while optimizing its risk management efforts.

It is vital to recognize that resource availability may change over time, and businesses should frequently examine and adapt their risk priority depending on the dynamic resource situation.

Emerging Risks

Effective risk management requires anticipating and resolving new hazards. Risks on the horizon or with the potential to evolve quickly may be prioritized to guarantee early detection and proactive mitigation. In a continually changing world, this enables firms to stay ahead of new dangers and grasp opportunities.

- Cybersecurity and Data Breaches: As technology progresses, cyber threats and data breaches evolve and become more sophisticated. New forms of malware, ransomware attacks, targeted hacking strategies and vulnerabilities in developing technologies such as Internet of Things (IoT) devices and cloud computing are among the rising concerns in this arena. These risks can result in major financial losses, damage to one's reputation, and the compromise of important customer or business data.

- Artificial Intelligence (AI) and Automation: Rapid AI, machine learning, and automation use bring both benefits and hazards. The ethical implications of AI decision-making, algorithm biases, employment displacement, and the possibility for AI systems to malfunction or be exploited are all emerging issues. To enable ethical AI use and to prevent any unforeseen repercussions, organizations must carefully traverse these risks.

- Climate Change and Environmental Risks: Climate change and the risks linked with it are receiving more attention. Extreme weather events, increasing sea levels, resource scarcity, and regulatory reforms aimed at lowering carbon emissions are all emerging dangers. These hazards can have an impact on a variety of industries, including agriculture, real estate, insurance, and energy, and may necessitate firms adapting their operations, supply networks, and business models.

- Geopolitical Uncertainty: Political and geopolitical events can generate new risks that have an influence on global businesses. Trade disputes, economic penalties, geopolitical wars, changes in government legislation, and political instability in certain regions are examples of such hazards. International organizations must monitor and assess these risks in order to secure their operations, investments, and supply networks.

- Technological Disruptions: Rapid technological breakthroughs can disrupt entire businesses and introduce new hazards. Blockchain technology, for example, has the potential to disrupt existing financial systems, while autonomous vehicles offer hazards to the transportation industry. To remain competitive and resilient, organizations must stay on top of technology upheavals and proactively manage the risks that come with them.

- Pandemics and Health crisis: The recent COVID-19 pandemic showed the global health crisis' influence on organizations around the world. The possibility for new infectious diseases, antibiotic resistance, and the weaknesses of global supply chains and transport networks are all emerging hazards in this field. To limit the effect of future health crises, organizations should build robust contingency plans and crisis response methods.

These instances demonstrate that emergent hazards can arise from a variety of sources and have far-reaching consequences for businesses. Businesses must constantly scan the external world, participate in scenario planning, and undertake risk assessments to identify and prepare for these developing hazards. By doing so, firms may successfully adapt, innovate, and respond to potential disruptions and embrace new possibilities.

It is important to remember that priority criteria may differ depending on the specific setting, industry, and organizational goals. Organizations should develop their own risk prioritizing criteria and weighting depending on their own circumstances and risk appetite. Organizations can efficiently allocate resources, handle significant risks proactively, and improve overall risk management efforts by considering these variables and adopting a systematic and consistent approach to risk prioritization.

Risk prioritization techniques

To assess and prioritize risks, qualitative approaches rely on subjective judgments and expert opinions. In qualitative assessments, techniques such as risk matrices, risk scoring, and risk classification are widely employed. This strategy ranks hazards based on their characteristics and assists in identifying risks that demand quick action.

Advantages of Qualitative Assessment

When compared to quantitative methods, qualitative assessment is often simpler and easier to understand. It does not necessitate complex computations or specialist data analysis abilities, allowing it to be used by a broader range of stakeholders. This ease of use allows for a faster assessment procedure, which is especially useful when dealing with a high number of hazards.

Qualitative evaluation enables for expert judgment and expertise to be included. This method considers the views and opinions of competent personnel with a thorough understanding of the business, its operations, and the hazards involved. Expert judgment can provide crucial insights that quantitative methods alone may not be able to capture.

Qualitative assessment allows for adaptation to various contexts and risk domains. It can be used in instances when there is a scarcity of data or historical information. It enables the assessment of a wide range of risk factors, including developing hazards or those that are difficult to correctly define.

Qualitative assessment promotes a holistic view of risks by considering a variety of qualitative elements such as the nature of the risk, its core causes, and its repercussions. This larger perspective aids in identifying interrelated hazards, connections, and underlying weaknesses that a strictly numerical study may miss.

There are, however, some potential disadvantages of qualitative evaluation:

Inadequate Precision: One of the key disadvantages of qualitative assessment is the inability to quantify precisely. Without quantifiable data, it can be difficult to compare and prioritize hazards appropriately. When numerous assessors are engaged, this might lead to subjective biases or contradictions.

Qualitative evaluation does not provide the amount of information and precision that quantitative methods do. It may not detect tiny differences in risk levels or allow for exact risk comparisons. This constraint can make it difficult to do advanced risk studies, such as cost-benefit analysis or quantitative risk modeling.

Qualitative evaluation frequently relies on descriptive terminology or qualitative scales that are vulnerable to interpretation. This can make communicating and documenting risk assessments difficult, especially when different stakeholders have varying degrees of understanding or expertise.

Communication ambiguity can have an impact on decision-making and the execution of risk-mitigation methods.

Qualitative assessment is primarily reliant on subjective judgment and qualitative data. It may not make appropriate use of quantitative or historical data provided to the organization. This can lead to missed opportunities to capitalize on data-driven insights, as well as incomplete or skewed risk assessments.

Comparing and prioritizing risks might be difficult without accurate numerical numbers. Qualitative assessments may have difficulty providing a clear evaluation of risks based on their relative importance or probable impact. This can make it difficult to deploy resources efficiently or make sound risk management judgments.

While qualitative risk assessment has limits, it can nevertheless be a useful tool when quantitative data is insufficient or a broader, expert-driven perspective is necessary. It is frequently used in conjunction with quantitative methodologies to provide a more comprehensive knowledge of hazards and to enhance decision-making processes.

Quantitative techniques

Quantitative techniques entail assigning numerical values to hazards using statistical data, models, and calculations. To estimate risks based on their likelihood and potential impact, techniques such as probabilistic modeling, Monte Carlo simulations, and decision trees are utilized. This strategy produces a more objective and quantifiable risk ranking.

Advantages of quantitative techniques

Quantitative methods offer a systematic and impartial method of risk appraisal. They can aid in removing biases and subjectivity that may appear in qualitative evaluations by relying on data and mathematical models. The analysis's credibility and dependability are improved by its objectivity.

Quantitative methods provide accurate and exact measurements and forecasts. Statistical models can compute prospective losses or benefits, measure risks, and predict probabilities. Organizations can distribute resources more efficiently and with more knowledge because of this precision.

Quantitative methods make use of data to offer insights and assist choices. They enable the analysis of big datasets and the discovery of patterns, trends, and correlations that might not be readily apparent using only qualitative techniques. Organizations can recognize potential hazards and take reasoned decisions thanks to this data-driven strategy.

Quantitative methods offer a consistent framework for evaluating risks and comparing them. Risks can be easily compared and prioritized by using numerical values and metrics, which facilitates consistent decision-making across various projects or sectors within an organization.

Quantitative techniques allow for the development of risk models and simulations that may be used to assess the possible impact of various scenarios. For example, Monte Carlo simulations can examine the probability distribution of outcomes and provide a range of probable outcomes, assisting in risk mitigation planning and resource allocation.

There are some disadvantages to quantitative techniques, as follows.

Quantitative approaches rely greatly on the availability and quality of data. Data that is inaccurate or incomplete might produce misleading results and faulty analyses. Obtaining trustworthy and relevant data can be difficult, especially for developing threats or complicated systems with limited historical data.

In order to simulate complicated systems or uncertainties, quantitative techniques frequently require assumptions and simplifications. These assumptions have the potential to create biases or mistakes into the analysis. It is necessary to critically assess the assumptions and consider their potential impact on the results.

Quantitative methodologies may overlook essential contextual information and qualitative elements that might influence risk assessments. Human judgment, expert opinions, and qualitative insights can all provide valuable perspectives that quantitative models cannot. It is critical to strike a balance between quantitative and qualitative factors.

Quantitative procedures demand a certain amount of technical competence to implement. Developing and using mathematical models, statistical analysis, and computing approaches can be difficult and time-consuming. To properly apply these strategies, organizations may need to invest in training or seek outside expertise.

Quantitative approaches frequently assume a steady and predictable environment. Risks, on the other hand, are intrinsically unknown and might change over time. Quantitative models may have difficulty accounting for rapidly changing conditions, new hazards, and unanticipated events. It is critical to update and alter quantitative evaluations on a frequent basis to reflect changing risk landscapes.

In conclusion, quantitative methodologies provide useful insights and precision in risk analysis and decision-making. They provide objective and data-driven methodologies that enable firms to estimate risks and effectively allocate resources. However, it is critical to recognize their limits, which include data constraints,

simplifications, and the requirement for contextual and qualitative considerations. Integrating quantitative and qualitative
assessments can aid in the development of a more comprehensive and rigorous risk management strategy.

Risk Scoring and Ranking

Risk scoring entails assigning risk scores or ratings based on
predetermined criteria. Impact, likelihood, time sensitivity, and
other relevant characteristics may be included in these criteria. Risks are then scored and ranked, with higher-scoring risks
regarded as more severe and requiring quick response.

There are several advantages of Risk Scoring and Ranking:

Risk scoring and ranking give a structured and systematic
approach for objectively comparing hazards. It becomes easier to
identify and evaluate hazards based on their severity and potential impact by assigning scores or rankings.

These strategies aid in risk prioritization by directing attention
and resources toward risks with higher scores or rankings. This
enables firms to better manage their limited resources by addressing the most serious threats first.

Risk scoring and ranking procedures give a consistent framework for evaluating risks across an organization's many projects,
departments, or business units. This consistency encourages consistency in risk management approaches and allows for
successful communication and decision-making.

Scoring and ranking make it easier to communicate risks to stakeholders in a clear and succinct manner. Risks can be presented

in a more clear and comparable manner using a standardized approach, allowing stakeholders to make informed decisions and take relevant measures.

Organizations can focus their efforts on establishing mitigation solutions for the most significant risks by prioritizing hazards. This proactive approach enables rapid risk response planning and implementation, lowering the frequency and severity of adverse events.

The disadvantages of risk scoring and ranking are as follows:

Methodologies for risk scoring and ranking may add subjectivity to the process. Individual biases or interpretations may influence the assigning of scores or rankings, potentially leading to conflicting findings. To reduce subjectivity, it is critical to set explicit norms and criteria.

Risk scoring and ranking approaches frequently entail the simplification and consolidation of complex risk data. This simplification can result in the loss of essential nuances and details, perhaps neglecting critical aspects of hazards that a scoring or ranking system cannot fully represent.

While risk score and ranking provide a relative comparison, they may not fully reflect quantitative components of risks, such as exact probability or financial impact. The use of discrete scores or ranks may oversimplify the underlying complexity of dangers, making proper assessment difficult.

Scoring and ranking techniques may fail to account for specific contextual aspects that determine risk importance. Different sectors, projects, or organizational cultures may necessitate tailored considerations that go beyond a typical scoring or ranking system.

Risks are not static and can change over time. Scoring and ranking may not represent the dynamic nature of hazards or account for changes in the risk environment appropriately. To guarantee continuing risk management efficacy, scores, and rankings must be reassessed and adjusted on a regular basis.

It is critical to understand that risk scoring and ranking should be utilized as complimentary techniques within a larger risk management framework. They should be used in conjunction with other qualitative and quantitative risk assessment methodologies to ensure a thorough awareness of risks and allow for well-informed decision-making.

Organizations can effectively exploit risk scoring and ranking methods while addressing their inherent inadequacies by acknowledging the benefits and limits of these methods.

Cost-Benefit Analysis

Risks can be prioritized in some situations based on a cost-benefit analysis. This method entails weighing the prospective expenses of addressing a risk against the potential benefits of risk mitigation. Risks with a greater benefit-to-cost ratio are prioritized.

The level of risk that a company is ready to accept in order to achieve its goals is referred to as risk appetite. Organizations can prioritize risks that exceed acceptable thresholds by setting risk appetite and tolerance levels, ensuring that resources are focused on controlling risks that go outside acceptable bounds.

Effective risk prioritizing necessitates a methodical approach that considers many aspects and involves key stakeholders. It is a continuous process that should be assessed and modified on a frequent basis as new risks emerge and existing risks change. By carefully prioritizing risks, organizations may address the most serious threats first, deploy resources more efficiently, and improve their overall risk management procedures.

Risk Mitigation

Risk mitigation is an important part of the risk management process since it tries to lower the likelihood and impact of potential risks on an organization or project. It entails developing and implementing plans, actions, and controls to reduce, eliminate, or transfer risks. Organizations may improve their resilience, safeguard their assets, and raise their chances of success by proactively managing risks.

Effective risk mitigation necessitates a systematic and complete approach that includes risk identification, analysis, evaluation, and response. It entails comprehending the existence and characteristics of risks, assessing their potential repercussions, and devising effective countermeasures.

Key Risk Mitigation Principles

Risk Avoidance

In certain circumstances, avoiding a danger entirely is the most efficient method to reduce it. This entails evaluating potential risks and making strategic decisions to avoid behaviors or situations that could expose the organization to serious hazards. While risk avoidance is not always practicable or practical, it is nonetheless an effective risk reduction approach when viable alternatives exist.

Risk Transfer

The financial or operational weight of risk is transferred to another party through risk transfer. This can be accomplished through a variety of means, including insurance policies, contracts, and outsourcing arrangements. Organizations can decrease their exposure and assign responsibility to parties better able to handle certain risks by shifting risks to external entities.

Risk Reduction

Risk reduction tries to reduce the possibility or impact of risk by applying procedures that target its underlying causes or contributing variables directly. This can include developing safety rules, strengthening security measures, increasing quality control processes, or putting in place redundancy systems. To effectively manage vulnerabilities, risk reduction solutions frequently include investments in resources, technology, training, or infrastructure.

Risk Contingency Planning

Risk contingency planning is creating predetermined reaction strategies that will be implemented when specific risks occur. This method enables companies to predict future scenarios and take action to mitigate the effect of risks when they materialize. In response to specific hazards, contingency plans often include roles and duties, communication protocols, resource allocation, and alternative tactics to be adopted.

Risk Monitoring and Review

Risk reduction is an ongoing process that necessitates constant monitoring and frequent evaluation. Organizations can identify developing risks, evaluate the efficacy of current controls, and adapt their strategy by routinely assessing the effectiveness of applied mitigation measures. This iterative process guarantees that risk reduction initiatives stay relevant and adaptable to changing conditions.

Challenges and Considerations

While risk reduction is critical for organizational resilience, there are various problems and factors to consider:

Trade-offs

Risk-mitigation solutions may include trade-offs such as higher expenses, less flexibility, or lengthier decision-making procedures. To avoid jeopardizing overall performance, it is critical to find a balance between risk reduction and other corporate objectives.

Uncertainty

Risk mitigation necessitates making informed decisions based on available knowledge, which may be ambiguous. Organizations must assess risks based on the best available evidence and keep their understanding up to current when new information becomes available.

Complexity

Organizations operate in complicated contexts with interrelated hazards that can have cascading repercussions. Effective risk mitigation necessitates a comprehensive awareness of these intricacies as well as the capacity to traverse interdependencies across multiple risk categories.

Changing Landscape

The risk landscape is dynamic and ever-changing. Existing hazards might evolve over time, and new risks can emerge. To effectively manage their exposures, organizations must remain watchful, adjust their risk mitigation methods, and anticipate future threats.

Risk mitigation is a critical component of risk management because it helps companies to address possible hazards and defend their interests in advance. Organizations can reduce the likelihood and impact of risks by implementing a variety of measures such as risk avoidance, transfer, reduction, and contingency planning. Risk mitigation needs a thorough awareness of the hazards, ongoing monitoring, and the willingness to react to changing circumstances. Organizations may strengthen their resilience, and decision- making, and develop a culture of risk awareness and preparedness by prioritizing risk mitigation.

CONCLUSION

In the expansive realm of cybersecurity, we embarked on a journey through the intricate tapestry of digital landscapes, where the evolution of technology intertwined with the complexities of human behavior.

Our exploration began with the foundational concept of cybersecurity—an essential shield against the myriad threats lurking in the virtual domain. Defined as the collective effort to safeguard digital assets, cybersecurity emerged as a crucial sentinel in the digital cityscape. It was a dynamic force, adapting to the ever-changing landscape of cyber threats that mirrored the challenges faced by a bustling city.

As we delved into the nuances of cybersecurity threats, we uncovered a world where the virtual and tangible intersected, where the human touch became both the target and the defender against malevolent forces. In the realm of network security, the basics unfolded as the architecture of the digital city—where the intricate web of connections formed the backbone of communication. Firewalls, intrusion detection, and prevention systems stood as the city's guardians, vigilant against unauthorized access and potential breaches. The landscape expanded further into the wireless realm, where securing networks became a paramount task in a city bustling with wireless signals. This journey took us through the landscape of malware and antivirus measures, a battleground where digital viruses mirrored their biological counterparts, and defenders strived to create virtual antibodies to protect the integrity of the digital ecosystem. As we navigated through the intricate tapestry of cybersecurity, the importance of robust password management became evident. Best practices for password creation stood as the keys to the digital gates, ensuring that only authorized individuals traversed the virtual city.

The landscape broadened into the multi-dimensional realm of multi-factor authentication, a fortress built on the principle that the more layers of defense, the more secure the city became. Privacy and security considerations then came to the forefront, weaving a narrative that went beyond mere protection, emphasizing the intrinsic value of privacy in the digital age.

The legal and ethical considerations of cybersecurity emerged as guiding principles in this digital cityscape, akin to the legal framework that upheld order and justice in physical societies. Cybercrime laws and regulations defined the rules of engagement, ensuring that the digital citizens adhered to ethical standards and legal obligations. Privacy laws and regulations became the civic code, safeguarding the digital citizens' rights to privacy and establishing boundaries for the responsible use of data. In the realm of information management, the importance of understanding, classifying, and safeguarding information became the cornerstone of responsible digital citizenship. Secure file transfer, information classification, and handling formed the protocols that dictated how information flowed through the digital city. These measures ensured that sensitive data remained protected, and the citizens had the tools to navigate the vast sea of information responsibly.

Physical security, a concept mirroring the protection of physical assets in the tangible world, became a pivotal aspect of cybersecurity. Access control for physical locations, surveillance, and monitoring, securing assets and equipment—all these components contributed to the overarching goal of creating a resilient digital infrastructure. Social engineering, the human element in this digital realm, unveiled the vulnerabilities that lay in the psyche of digital citizens. Understanding and preventing social engineering attacks became essential skills, akin to building immunity against psychological manipulation in the physical world. Cryptography and encryption formed the digital codes and ciphers that secured the communication lines in our virtual city. This intricate dance of algorithms and keys ensured that confidential information remained unreadable to unauthorized eyes. The principles of risk management, incident response, and disaster recovery became the emergency services of our digital city, ready to tackle crises and ensure continuity in the face of adversity. As we navigated through this digital cityscape, the landscape unfolded with the emergence of new threats and trends. Cybersecurity became a dynamic force, adapting to the ever- evolving challenges posed by the digital landscape. The Internet of Things (IoT) introduced a new dimension, where the city expanded into a vast network of interconnected devices.

The security of the IoT became synonymous with securing the very fabric of this extended digital city. In conclusion, our journey through the diverse realms of cybersecurity painted a vivid picture of a digital cityscape where technology and humanity coexisted. It was a landscape where defenders tirelessly strived to protect the integrity and well-being of digital citizens. In this dynamic city, the principles of education, collaboration, and a human-centric approach emerged as the pillars that fortified the digital realm against the ever-present threats. As we continued to navigate this evolving landscape, the essence of cybersecurity lay not only in the tools and technologies but in the shared responsibility of creating a secure and resilient digital future for all.